Memoirs of the Chevalier de St. George: with some private passages of the life of ... King James II. never before publish'd.

Prince of Wales James

PRINT EDITIONS

Eighteenth Century
Collections Online
Print Editions

Gale ECCO Print Editions

Relive history with *Eighteenth Century Collections Online*, now available in print for the independent historian and collector. This series includes the most significant English-language and foreign-language works printed in Great Britain during the eighteenth century, and is organized in seven different subject areas including literature and language; medicine, science, and technology; and religion and philosophy. The collection also includes thousands of important works from the Americas.

The eighteenth century has been called "The Age of Enlightenment." It was a period of rapid advance in print culture and publishing, in world exploration, and in the rapid growth of science and technology – all of which had a profound impact on the political and cultural landscape. At the end of the century the American Revolution, French Revolution and Industrial Revolution, perhaps three of the most significant events in modern history, set in motion developments that eventually dominated world political, economic, and social life.

In a groundbreaking effort, Gale initiated a revolution of its own: digitization of epic proportions to preserve these invaluable works in the largest online archive of its kind. Contributions from major world libraries constitute over 175,000 original printed works. Scanned images of the actual pages, rather than transcriptions, recreate the works *as they first appeared.*

Now for the first time, these high-quality digital scans of original works are available via print-on-demand, making them readily accessible to libraries, students, independent scholars, and readers of all ages.

For our initial release we have created seven robust collections to form one the world's most comprehensive catalogs of 18ᵗʰ century works.

Initial Gale ECCO Print Editions collections include:

History and Geography
Rich in titles on English life and social history, this collection spans the world as it was known to eighteenth-century historians and explorers. Titles include a wealth of travel accounts and diaries, histories of nations from throughout the world, and maps and charts of a world that was still being discovered. Students of the War of American Independence will find fascinating accounts from the British side of conflict.

Social Science

Delve into what it was like to live during the eighteenth century by reading the first-hand accounts of everyday people, including city dwellers and farmers, businessmen and bankers, artisans and merchants, artists and their patrons, politicians and their constituents. Original texts make the American, French, and Industrial revolutions vividly contemporary.

Medicine, Science and Technology

Medical theory and practice of the 1700s developed rapidly, as is evidenced by the extensive collection, which includes descriptions of diseases, their conditions, and treatments. Books on science and technology, agriculture, military technology, natural philosophy, even cookbooks, are all contained here.

Literature and Language

Western literary study flows out of eighteenth-century works by Alexander Pope, Daniel Defoe, Henry Fielding, Frances Burney, Denis Diderot, Johann Gottfried Herder, Johann Wolfgang von Goethe, and others. Experience the birth of the modern novel, or compare the development of language using dictionaries and grammar discourses.

Religion and Philosophy

The Age of Enlightenment profoundly enriched religious and philosophical understanding and continues to influence present-day thinking. Works collected here include masterpieces by David Hume, Immanuel Kant, and Jean-Jacques Rousseau, as well as religious sermons and moral debates on the issues of the day, such as the slave trade. The Age of Reason saw conflict between Protestantism and Catholicism transformed into one between faith and logic -- a debate that continues in the twenty-first century.

Law and Reference

This collection reveals the history of English common law and Empire law in a vastly changing world of British expansion. Dominating the legal field is the *Commentaries of the Law of England* by Sir William Blackstone, which first appeared in 1765. Reference works such as almanacs and catalogues continue to educate us by revealing the day-to-day workings of society.

Fine Arts

The eighteenth-century fascination with Greek and Roman antiquity followed the systematic excavation of the ruins at Pompeii and Herculaneum in southern Italy; and after 1750 a neoclassical style dominated all artistic fields. The titles here trace developments in mostly English-language works on painting, sculpture, architecture, music, theater, and other disciplines. Instructional works on musical instruments, catalogs of art objects, comic operas, and more are also included.

The BiblioLife Network

This project was made possible in part by the BiblioLife Network (BLN), a project aimed at addressing some of the huge challenges facing book preservationists around the world. The BLN includes libraries, library networks, archives, subject matter experts, online communities and library service providers. We believe every book ever published should be available as a high-quality print reproduction; printed on-demand anywhere in the world. This insures the ongoing accessibility of the content and helps generate sustainable revenue for the libraries and organizations that work to preserve these important materials.

The following book is in the "public domain" and represents an authentic reproduction of the text as printed by the original publisher. While we have attempted to accurately maintain the integrity of the original work, there are sometimes problems with the original work or the micro-film from which the books were digitized. This can result in minor errors in reproduction. Possible imperfections include missing and blurred pages, poor pictures, markings and other reproduction issues beyond our control. Because this work is culturally important, we have made it available as part of our commitment to protecting, preserving, and promoting the world's literature.

GUIDE TO FOLD-OUTS MAPS and OVERSIZED IMAGES

The book you are reading was digitized from microfilm captured over the past thirty to forty years. Years after the creation of the original microfilm, the book was converted to digital files and made available in an online database.

In an online database, page images do not need to conform to the size restrictions found in a printed book. When converting these images back into a printed bound book, the page sizes are standardized in ways that maintain the detail of the original. For large images, such as fold-out maps, the original page image is split into two or more pages

Guidelines used to determine how to split the page image follows:

• Some images are split vertically; large images require vertical and horizontal splits.
• For horizontal splits, the content is split left to right.
• For vertical splits, the content is split from top to bottom.
• For both vertical and horizontal splits, the image is processed from top left to bottom right.

MEMOIRS

OF THE

Chevalier *de* St. GEORGE:

With some

PRIVATE PASSAGES

OF THE

LIFE

Of the late

King *JAMES* II.

Never before publish'd.

Rapin xviii.

LONDON:

Printed in the Year M DCC XII.
(Price One Shilling.)

MEMOIRS

OF THE

Chevalier *de St. George*, &c.

WHATEVER the Reader may conceive under this *Romantic* Title, I muſt ask his Pardon, for ſome few Pages at leaſt, to be a little ſerious · As to the Original of this Young *Hero*, let him take it as it ſtands in Hiſtory, without putting me to the trouble of aſcertaining, that either the *Chevalier De St. George* is *James* III. or *James* III. Son of *James* II. Something therefore relative to theſe Memoirs, let me ſay of his (ſuppos'd or pretended) Father, ſince I ſhall elſe begin a Structure without any Foundation at all, which would ſeem a very Miraculous as well as Unaccountable piece of Work.

I cannot remember, that ever *England* had a fairer Sunſhine, or Proſpect of Happineſs, than at the joyful RESTORATION of the Royal Family ; when after a long and unnatural Exile, they were reſtor'd to their law-

B ful

ful Rights and Honours. The Reign fucceeding I fhall not meddle with, nor pretend to decide whether it was the Prince or the People that occafion'd the domeftic Troubles that were then Predominant, yet this I think I am oblig'd to fay, and which all reafonable Men will I believe own, That the Exile I have Mention'd was the grand Motive, or Foundation of all the Troubles we have undergone fince.

The Queen Mother, who was banifh'd with her Children, took care to infpire them early with favorable Sentiments of her own Religion, and to diffipate the Prejudice of former Education. What effect it had on the reft, I cannot exactly fay, but on the Duke of *York* it took fuch Root, that together with his Correfpondence with the *Catholicks* in *Flanders*, contributed to ftrengthen the immoveable Impreffions he had receiv'd of the Truth of the *Catholic* Religion.

After his Return to *England*, he foon made himfelf beloved and refpected by the Nobility and Gentry; nor did he want a fufficient fhare of Intereft in the Hearts of the Common People. He commanded the Navy againft the *Dutch*, and in Two Engagements fufficiently rais'd his Reputation: But this Profperity did not laft long, for without any Eclipfe of his Merit, he began to decline in the Hearts of the People; when they perceiv'd that either he had chang'd his Religion, or, at leaft, had a mind to do it: And what added to it was the Sufpicion likewife that he had converted the Dutchefs his Firft Wife, who dy'd in the infancy of thefe Rumors, which therefore leffen'd sen'd the impression it began to make on the People. And they were yet in some hopes for the Duke himself; but he had 'ere this made his Abjuration to Father *Simons* an *English Jesuit*. And tho' the measures he took were always most Prudent, and he did not publickly declare himself to be a *Catholic*, 'twas nevertheless mighty difficult with him, not to discover to the *Protestants*, that he had separated from their Communion.

The Parliament took the Alarm, and from that time Measures were contriv'd to alter the Right of Succession. There were some Bishops of the Church of *England*, who foreseeing the Effect of so violent a Proceeding, would have stopp'd the Blow ; to which end they addressed themselves to the Duke himself. They begg'd of him only to accompany the King his Brother to Chappel, when His Majesty went to the *Protestant* Prayers: They humbly represented to him, that such a wise Proceeding might lay the Tempest that had been rais'd against him, and prevent the Bill of *Exclusion* from making its way thro' the Parliament. But they cou'd not prevail with him, receiving for Answer, these Words,— *My Principles do not suffer me to dissemble my Religion after that manner ; and I cannot obtain of my self to do Evil that Good may come of it.*

This Constancy of the Duke's threw the King into such disorder, that he had very great need of all his Authority and Force: For as he had a tender love for him, he was mov'd with the Danger wherein he saw him; resolving to support him against the Tor-

rent

rent of his Enemies, which ịu the main he did; neverthelefs the Duke found himfelf oblig'd to refign his Place of *Grand* Admiral, and his other Trufts: Thofe who ftuck the clofeft to him before, remov'd themfelves from his Perfon; and this unhappy Prince, who was Prefumptive Heir to Three Kingdoms, and had been us'd to behold a Crowd of admiring Courtiers about him, was of a fudden reduced to the Condition of a Private Perfon, and abandon'd by all the World.

Yet fo far did the King's Endearments go, and the better to prevent the Alteration of the Succeffion to the Crown, that he of himfelf propofed to the Duke of *York* a Second Marr age. As his Majefty had no Legitimate Children, and indeed defpairing of ever attaining that Bleffing; he judg'd it convenient that his Brother who had but Two Daughters left, fhou'd have an HEIR, who might one day fit on the Throne of *England*. The Princefs thought on by His Majefty, was the Lady *Mary d' Efte*, Sifter to *Francis*, Duke of *Modena*, and Daughter to *Alphonfo D' Efte*, the Third of that Name, Duke of *Modena*, by Madam *Laura Martineffi*, his Wife She was born upon the 25th of *September*, *Anno* 1658, and had not paffed the 15th Year of her Age, when at *Modena* fhe was Marry'd to His Royal Highnefs, by his Proxy, *Henry*, Earl of *Peterborough*, who with a noble Retinue attended Her Highnefs and the Dutchefs Dowager her Mother into *France*, and after having refided fome time at *Paris*, they came to *Calais*, and thence

t

to *Dover*, where they arrived *Nov.* 21ſt, 1673. At *Dover* ſhe was receiv'd by the Duke, where the Marriage betwixt them was perſonately Conſummated by the Right Reverend Father in God, Dr. *Nathaniel Crew*, Lord Biſhop of *Durham*, and now Lord *Crew*.

At *London* they were entertain'd with high Reſpect at the Court of *England*, where the Dutcheſs Dowager, her Mother, having continued about the ſpace of 6 Weeks, in order for the Settlement of her Daughter, ſhe return'd to *Italy*, to manage Affairs in the Infancy of the Duke her Son.

This Marriage met with great Oppoſition on the part of the Parliament, becauſe the Princeſs was a *Roman Catholic*, yet the King gave little regard to what was Remonſtrated to him on that account. He was pleaſed after, that the Dutcheſs prov'd fruitful, from whence he hoped a numerous Progeny to ſupply the Throne, which he judg'd in time would eat up and deſtroy all manner of Prejudice. And here I think it will not be improper to repeat the Iſſue ſhe had by the Duke, before the Perſon I am writing of, was ſaid to be born.

On the 10th of *January*, 1674, ſhe was brought to bed of a Daughter, at the Palace of St *James's*. She was Baptis'd by the Name of *Katherina Laura*, having for Godmothers the Ladies *Mary* and *Anne*, her Half Siſters, and the Duke of *Monmouth* for her Godfather. She dy'd the Year following, *Anno* 1675, on the 3d of *October*; and was interr'd in the Vault of *Mary*, Queen of *Scotland*.

Iſabella,

Isabella of *York*, Second Daughter of His (then) Royal Highness, *James*, Duke of *York*, and the Lady *Mary D'Este*, his Second Wife, was born at St. *James's*, the 28th of *August*, *Anno* 1676. Her Godmothers were the Dutchess of *Monmouth* and the Countess of *Peterborough*, and her Godfather, *Thomas*, Earl of *Danby*, Lord High Treasurer of *England*, now Duke of *Leeds*. This young Princess dy'd at the Age of 3 Years, 6 Months, and Odd Days, *viz.* the 2d of *March* 1680, and was privately bury'd in the Vault of *Mary*, Queen of *Scots*.

Charles of *York*, Duke of *Cambridge*, first Son of His Royal Highness, *James*, Duke of *York*, by the Lady *Mary D'Este* his second Wife, was born at St. *James's*, the 7th of *November*, *Anno* 1677, and the Next Day Baptis'd by the Bishop of *Durham*; the King his Uncle, and the Prince of *Orange*, were his Godfathers, and the Lady *Isabella* his Sister his Godmother. He dy'd suddenly on the 12th of *December* the same Year, and was interr'd privately in the Tomb of *Mary*, Queen of *Scots*

Charlot Maria of *York*, third Daughter of *James*, Duke of *York*, by the Lady *Mary D'Este* his second Wife, was born at St. *James's* the 15th of *August* 1682, and 2 Days after was christen'd by *Henry*, Bishop of *London*. Her Godmothers were the Countesses of *Arundel* and *Clarendon*; and the Duke of *Ormond* her Godfather. She dy'd the 6th of *October* following, and was interr'd privately in the Vault of *Mary*, Queen of *Scots*.

None

None of thefe Children furviving long, gave wings to the Ambition of the Duke's Enemies; but had a contrary effect on the King's Spirits, and thofe who had any efteem for him. Another thing now trump'd up, that mightily help'd to overwhelm the Duke's Intereft, and alleviate even the good Opinion the King had of him, and this was the *Popifh* Plot, wherein the Duke was brought in. The Accufers boldly gave out, that they were firft to have affaulted the King's perfon, and after that to have made away with all the *Proteftants*. The Parliament took the Alarm and encourag'd the Difcovery of it; and the King when he met them, told them in his Speech; " That he had been inform'd " of a Defign againft his Perfon, by the *Je-* " *fuits*, whereupon a Bill was brought in, " and pafs'd into an Act, *For the more ef-* *fectual preferving the King's Perfon and Govern-* *ment, by difabling* Papifts *from fitting in either* *Houfe of Parliament.* Five of the *Popifh* Lords were committed to the *Tower*, and impeach'd of High Treafon, One of which was beheaded. Diligent fearch was made after the Priefts, and the Religious, feveral of them were hang'd up in *London*, and others dy'd miferably in the Prifons they were fent to.

The King however was very unwilling to lend an ear to the Sufpicions rais'd againft his Brother, and therefore did all he cou'd to endeavor to clear him of the Infinuations laid againft him: The Duke defpis'd the fcandalous Difcourfes, and falfe Reports that were made of him : But he was little fenfible of the preffing Inftances, and indeed the *Re-*

proaches

proaches of his Friends, who carry'd 'em fo far, as to condemn the firm Steddinefs of his Mind, giving it the Name of *Prejudice,* and *Obftinacy in Opinion.* They remonftrated to him, that he wou'd be the occafion of his own, and the King's Ruin, and the utter Extinction of the *Catholic* Faith in *England;* and the Overthrow of the State. A greater Check he yet met with from the King, who urg'd his Reafons with great Strength, and earneftly begg'd him to be contented to keep his Religion in his own Breaft, without dif-covering and giving open Proofs of it to the World, who at fuch a juncture wou'd not fail to improve it to his Ruin. He likewife remonftrated to him the great Hardfhips they had undergone already from the implacable, Temper of the *Englifh* Nation, and conclu-ded all with affuring him he fhould never want his Protection, did he not put it out of his power to cherifh and fupport him. But the Duke remain'd inflexible, and re folv'd to hazard all, rather than diffemble his Religion

The King, on the other hand, finding fome-thing muft of neceffity be done to appeafe the Minds of the People, thought fit to have the Duke remove to *Bruffels,* and after fome Months or der'd him to pafs into *Scotland.* He obey'd the King with an entire Submiffion, and inftantly prepar'd to be gone But it was a fmart Trial with a Heart fo tender as his, to take leave of the King on thefe Conditions.

On the other hand, he found the King fof ten'd into Tears, and the Dutchefs his Con fort Inconfolable on this occafion. Neverthe lef less he still bore up against his own Tenderness, and the violent Motions of Nature that work'd so strongly on his Mind, and so without Trouble or Complaint set out as the King had commanded him.

During his residence in *Scotland*, he sufficiently won upon the Hearts of the People, and the Parliament there by a solemn Deputation return'd their most humble Thanks to His Majesty, that he had sent them a Prince so very acceptable to them: Which favorable Account made way for his Return into *England* a Few Months after.

In the Year 1680, a New Parliament being call'd, the Commons fell into a debate of the *Popish* Plot, and came to several vigorous resolutions, the First of which was against the Duke of *York* as being a *Papist*; and after several Speeches it was resolv'd that a Bill shou'd be brought in (this was the Second Bill of *Exclusion*) to disable *James*, Duke of *York*, from inheriting the Imperial Crown of *England*, and *Ireland*, and the Dominions thereunto belonging: Which Bill pass'd the Lower House, and was carry'd up to the Lords by *William* Lord *Russel*, but at the second reading the Lords threw it out · And the King, upon the Warmth that grew in Parliament, found himself oblig'd to dissolve them. Soon after the King calling a New Parliament to meet at *Oxford*, a Third Bill of *Exclusion* was brought in, read the first time, and order'd a Second Reading, but the King thought fit again to prorogue them. Soon after the Duke return'd to *England*, where he was receiv'd in a very affectionate manner by

C the

King; and the Act drawn up against him was no more talk'd of.

The Duke's Friends had now in their turn an Instance of Triumph, in the Discovery of the *Ryehouse* Plot, for which several of his most inveterate Enemies suffer'd Death, and others were sufficiently mortify'd. From whence to the Death of his Brother King *Charles* II and his attaining the Crown, he had a clearer sunshine of Peace, than the Foregoing Part of his Life had been acquainted with : Nor shall I omit one Passage at his Brother's Decease, which is borrow'd from an * Author, who seems to   * *Father* Francis
be of Credit.   Brettoneau's *A-*

   " As his Zeal was ever the *bridgment of the*
" same in Adversity, so he *Life of K.* James II.
" took care to preserve it in Prosperity
" He passionately desir'd the King's Conver-
" sion, and found it pretty well advanc'd,
" when he came to discourse the King on
" such Occasions as he thought most seasona-
" ble.

   " The King gave him a Paper he had com-
" pos'd himself, and writ with his own
" Hand, which contain'd a Summary of the
" most Material and Solid Arguments for the
" Truth of the *Catholic* Religion. In fine,
" Heaven gave a blessing to these good Dis-
" positions, and the Duke had this Comfort
" when he lost his Brother, to see him dy
" in the Bosom of the True Church.

   " King *Charles* II. fell sick, and on the 4th
" Day of his Illness, was by his Physicians gi
" ven over: When Two *Protestant* Bishop
" came to wait on His Majesty, they begar
                               " to

" to read, as is ufual, at the Bed's Feet, the
" Office for the Vifitation of the Sick.
" When they came to the Place where the
" Sick Perfon is exhorted to make Auricular
" Confeffion, but at the fame time is told,
" that there's no Command obliges him to it,
" and he may if he pleafes difpence with it;
" the Bifhop of *Bath* ftepp'd up to the King,
" made him a fhort Exhortation, and ask'd
" him if he repented of his Sins? The King
" having anfwer'd, *He did fo*; His Lordfhip
" pronounc'd the Form of Abfolution, after
" the Manner of the Church of *England*.'
" When the Office was over, the Bifhop re-
" turn'd to the King to ask him whether he
" was willing to receive the Sacrament; and
" to exhort him to it. But the King an-
" fwer'd him not a Word. His Lordfhip
" urg'd, and the King was pleas'd to tell him
" he would think on't. The Bifhop ftill in-
" fifting on it, His Majefty ftill evaded it.

" The Duke of *York* did not let flip fo fine
" an Occafion. He order'd all thofe who
" were by the King's Bedfide to withdraw;
" and then addreffing himfelf to the King,
" he teftify'd his Joy to fee him at laft (as he
" thought) refolv'd to execute what his Con-
" fcience had fo often follicited him to do;
" and offer'd at the fame time to call for a
" Prieft. *For God's fake Brother*, anfwer'd
" the King, *go fend for one*. But added he,
" *Won't you expofe your felf too much?* To
" which the Duke reply'd, *Sir, tho' it fhou'd*
" *coft me my Life, I will get you one*. He went
" out immediately, and by a particular Acci-
" dent, or a very fingular Providence, the

C 2   " Firft

" First Prieſt he met was Father *Huddleſtone*
" a *Benedictine*, the ſame that contributed
" much towards the Saving the King's Life
" after the Battle of *Worceſter*, when that
" Prince hid himſelf all Night in the Hollow
" of a Tree. Father *Huddleſtone* was ſhew'd
" up a Private pair of Stairs into a Cloſet
" near the King's Bedchamber. As ſoon as
" the King knew him, he gave order for all
" that were in the Chamber to retire, except
" his Brother.

" The Duke however had a mind that the
" Earl of *Bath*, Firſt Gentleman of the Bed-
" chamber, and the Earl of *Feverſham*, Cap-
" tain of the Guards, both *Proteſtants*, ſhou'd
" ſtay and be Witneſs of what paſt. This
" Precaution he thought neceſſary to prevent
" the malignant Conſequences that his Ene-
" mies might have made from thence, in caſe
" the Duke had ſtaid alone with the King,
" when His Majeſty was in that weak condi-
" tion.

" Father *Huddleſtone* went in, receiv'd the
" King's Abjuration, heard his Confeſſion, and
" afterwards adminiſter'd him the Sacraments.
" There was no delaying the Matter, for a few
" Hours after the King dy'd. He acknowledg'd
" upon his Death-Bed, that next to God, he
" ow'd the Grace of his Reconciliation to the
" *Church*, to the indefatigable Zeal and tender
" Affection of the Duke his Brother. Nay more,
" he ask'd his Pardon aloud for the ſevere
" Treatment he had ſeveral times given him ;
" and teſtify'd to thoſe who were preſent, in
" terms of Eſteem, Friendſhip, and Tenderneſs
" not to be expreſs'd, how much he was touch'd
                                                    " with

" with the Resignation and Patience which
" the Duke had all along shewn on those Oc-
" casions.

After the Death of King *Charles* II. the
Duke of *York* was proclaim'd King of *Great
Britain*, by the Name of *James* II. Publick Re-
joicings were heard in all Cities; and the Acclamations, and Shouts of Joy, which were
heard from all parts, gave occasion to hope for
a very happy Reign both to Prince and People.
If he had follow'd the Advice of his Council, he wou'd have been a little remiss in the
point of Religion: They wou'd have persua-
ded him to stay some time before he publickly
declar'd himself a *Catholic.* Of this opinion
were several *Catholicks* themselves; but all the
Reasons they offer'd him, made no manner of
impression on his Mind, and the *Sunday* after
his accession to the Crown he heard Mass publickly.

Not fully content with this Proceeding, he
design'd to re-establish Liberty of Conscience
in *England* by Act of Parliament, wherein
the *Catholicks* should be comprehended, as well
as the rest of the Nonconformists; mean time
he gave it out beforehand, as some of the
ablest Lawyers after serious Examination, af-
sur'd he might by Virtue of his *Prerogative
Royal.*

The present Juncture was favorable enough
for the King to make his Orders obey'd, and
execute what he had undertaken, as to Liberty of Conscience. One wou'd have thought
that the Defeat of the Duke of *Monmouth*,
and the Earl of *Argyle*, who took up Arms,
one in *England*, and the other in *Scotland*,
                                          shou'd

fhou'd have confirm'd his Authority. But the Prejudice to the *Catholic* Religion had fo deeply prevail'd in the Hearts of the People, that it foon rais'd new Troubles, and hinder'd the King's Intentions.

It was infinuated to the People, that the King defign'd to deftroy the Church of *England*, and introduce *Popery*, by main Force; that their Liberties and Properties were in danger, and themfelves of being opprefs'd by an Arbitrary Government. Thefe Reports eat into the Peoples Minds, and there lay corroding; and from that time nothing but Complaints and Murmurings were heard over all the Nation: After all the moft Moderate Men confefs'd, that excepting the Cafe of Religion, they cou'd not wifh for a King fitter to procure the Advantage of the Nation, both in refpect to his perfonal Vertues, and of his great Infight in Trade and Government.

Whilft Affairs were at this Crifis, the Queen, who had already had Four Children, as we have mention'd, was now with child, and fufficient caufe of Joy it was to the King's Friends, efpecially the *Catholicks*. A Proclamation was publifh'd appointing a public Day of Thankfgiving to be obferv'd in the Cities of *London* and *Weftminfter*, and foon after in all other Places of the Kingdom, and a fuitable Form of Prayer was likewife order'd to be prepar'd for that purpofe.

This News caus'd various Reflections thro'out the Nation, and inftead of allaying the former heat of the People, enflam'd them the more. They entertain'd a Prejudice, which no doubt was initill'd into them, that the Queen

Queen's Big Belly was only a Feint, an Artifice of the *R. Catholicks*, for some end or other; but yet they knew not what Name to give it. And as every thing seem'd to forward the King's Misfortunes, about this time the Bishops were sent to the *Tower*, a Proceeding the King was more to blame in, than the Blackest Incidents they had to charge him with.

On the 10th of *June*, between the Hours of 9 and 10, a Rumor spread that the Queen was in labor; the Town took the alarm, and People seem'd not a little surpris'd. This was not only confirm'd, but was soon follow'd with the News of her being brought to bed of a Prince, and in the Afternoon the following Account was publish'd by Authority.

" *Whitehall, June* 10. This day between 9
" and 10 in the Morning, the Queen was
" safely deliver'd of a Prince at St. *James*'s;
" His Majesty, the Queen Dowager, most of
" the Lords of the Privy Council, and di-
" vers Ladies of Quality being by.

' The Prince of *Orange* himself, and the States of *Holland*, sent to compliment the King upon this Occasion, and acknowledg'd the new Prince, as did almost all the Cities in the Kingdom, who thereupon presented their Addresses to His Majesty, full of Expressions that signify'd a most sincere Fidelity and Zeal. Notwithstanding which there was a very deep Resentment lay hid in the Breasts of most People. The Prepossession they had that the Prince was imposed on them, was agitated by other melancholy Circumstances; that the Order of the Church and Constitu-

tion

tion were in danger of being totally fub-
verted: And this, as a ftronger Phyfic on
the Mind, drove out all leffer Humors,
and divefted them even of the Refpect and
Allegiance they ow'd to their Sovereign. It un-
luckily happen'd too, that Five Days after this
Account was publifh'd of the Birth of the
Prince, the Bifhops were brought to Trial,
and the Army lay then encamp'd at *Hounflow
Heath* · Two things which did grievoufly
alarm and afflict the People: The former
needed no Aggravation of Words to pro-
voke them, the Trial was public, and as univerfally refented: The other required a little
Art to poffefs them, that it was an *Irifh Ca-
tholic-Army,* and defigned to keep a heavy
hand over the Kingdom, if they pretended
to difpute the King's Authority in repealing
the *Tefts* and *Penal Laws,* by which Method
he defigned to introduce his own Religion.

This work'd fo effectually, that People
were every where ripe for *Self-Defence,* and
the King was no lefs than accus'd of impofing
a Child for his Lawful Succeffor, to the prejudice of his own Daughters, for whom he had
always exprefs'd all the Affection and Tender-
nefs imaginable, and they to him, and paid all
the Duty and Refpect d : to an indulgent Father   And notwithftanding all the Royal Fa-
vors he had beftow'd, yet he found he cou'd
depend on nothing but his Army; nor with
any great Confidence on them, which made
him refolve to try how far he might truft to
their Fidelity, and therefore endeavor'd to
engage them, both Officers and Soldiers, to
fign a Writing, whereby they fhou'd promife
to

to contribute as far as in them lay, towards supporting the King's Design of taking off the *Test* and *Penal* Laws. This Project was thought fit to be propos'd to all the Regiments one by one, and the first, His Majesty's Desires were made known to, was the Earl of *Litchfield*'s Regiment, who all thereupon, both Officers and Soldiers (Two Captains and some private Men excepted) laid down their Arms; at which the King being astonish'd, commanded them to take up their Arms again. This was a sufficient Experiment of the Temper of the Soldiers; and His Majesty found that nothing but new modelling the Army would do.

Things standing in this disposition, a *Memorial* of the *Church* of *England* was drawn up privately, and sent to the Prince and Princess of *Orange*, to implore their Protection, whilst many of the Nobility and Gentry join'd in these Sollicitations; and others withdrew themselves into *Holland*, where they gave the Prince Assurances of a sufficient Power, that wou'd immediately join him on his landing.

In the mean time, His Majesty had resolv'd to call a Free Parliament, to establish an Universal Liberty of Conscience, and to remedy all the Complaints of his Subjects. The Charter of the City of *London* was restor'd, the Suspension of the Bishop of *London* taken off, the Deputy Lieutenants and Justices of the Peace, who had been remov'd for disputing His Majesty's Commands, were suffer'd to resume their Commissions; and a Proclamation

D was

was publifh'd for reftoring Corporations to their ancient Charters.

The Rumor of the Prince's being an Impoftor, began to fpread with greater Warmth, and to this was added, that his true Mother was to be brought over with the *Dutch* Fleet: Being now about Four Months old, he received private baptifm in the Chappel of St. *James*'s, on the 15th of of *October*, of which the Following Account was publifh'd by Authority.

" *Whitehal, Oct.* 15. This day, in the
" Chappel of St. *James*'s, His Royal High-
" nefs the Prince of *Wales*, being before
" chriften'd, was folemnly nam'd (amidft the
" Ceremonies and Rites of Baptifm) *James*
" *Francis, Edward.* His Holinefs, repre
fented by his Nuntio, Godfather, and the Queen Dowager Godmother. The King and Queen affifted at the Solemnity, with a great Attendance of Nobility and Gentry and a Concourfe of People, all expreffing joy and fatisfaction, fuitable to the Place and Occafion.

And now to ftifle the Sufpicion and Report, which had gain'd but too much credit that the Prince was not lawfully born of the Queen's Body, the King affembled an Extraordinary Council, where the Queen Dowager, the Peers that were in Town both Spiritual and Temporal, the Lord Mayor and Aldermen, the Judges, and His Majefty's Council at Law, were prefent.

To

To whom His Majesty deliver'd himself in
this manner,

" My Lords,

"I Have call'd you together upon a very
" extraordinary Occasion; but extra-
" ordinary Diseases must have extraordinary
" Remedies The malicious Endeavors of
" my Enemies have so poison'd the Minds of
" some of my Subjects, that by the Reports
" I have from all hands, I have reason to be-
" lieve, that very many do not think this Son,
" with which it hath pleas'd God to bless me,
" to be mine, but a Suppos'd Child. But I
" may say, that by particular Providence,
" scarce any Child was ever born, where
" there were so many Persons present.
" I have taken this time to have the Mat-
" ter heard and examin'd here, expecting
" that the Prince of *Orange*, with the first
" Easterly Wind will invade this Kingdom:
" And as I have often ventur'd my Life for
" the Nation before I came to the Crown, so
" I think my self more oblig'd to do the same
" now I am King, and do intend to go in
" person against him, whereby I may be ex-
" pos'd to Accidents, and therefore I
" thought it necessary to have this now
" done, in order to satisfy the Minds of my
" Subjects, and to prevent this Kingdom be-
" ing engag'd in Blood and Confusion after my
" Death, desiring to do always what may
" contribute most to the Ease and Quiet of
" my People, which I have shew'd by secu-
" ring to them their Liberty of Conscience,
" and

" and the Enjoyment of their Properties,
" which I will always preserve.

" I have defir'd the Queen Dowager to
" give her felf the trouble to come hither,
" to declare what fhe knows concerning the
" Birth of my Son; and moft of the Ladies,
" Lords, and other Perfons who were pre-
" fent, are ready here to depofe upon Oath
" their knowledge of this Matter.

After His Majefty had ended his Speech
the Queen Dowager rifing from her Chair
which was placed on the King's Right Hand
was pleas'd to declare in the manner following.

" THAT when the King fent for her t
　　　　" the Queen's Labor, fhe came a
" foon as fhe cou'd, and never ftirr'd fror
" her till fhe was deliver'd of the Prince c
" *Wales.* To which fhe fign'd

　　　　　　　　　　　　Catherina

The Clerk of the Council was then o
der'd to receive the Oaths of the Ladie
Lords, and other Perfons, who had any ev
dence to deliver in this Matter.

Thefe were

THE Marchionefs　　The Countefs
　　of *Powis.*　　　　*Sunderland.*
The Countefs of　　The Countefs
Arran.　　　　　　*Rofcommon.*
The Countefs of　　The Countefs
Peterborow.　　　　*Fingal.*
　　　　　　　　　　The Lady *Bulkle*
　　　　　　　　　　　　　　　T

The Lady *Belasyse*.

The Lady *Waldgrave*.

Mrs. *Mary Crane* and Mrs. *Anne Cary*, Gentlewomen of the Bedchamber to Queen Dowager.

Mrs. *Isabella Wentworth*, Mrs. *Catherine Sayer*, Mrs. *Isabella Waldgrave*, Mrs. *Margaret Dawson*, Mrs. *Eliz. Bromley*, Mrs. *Pelegrina Turini*, Gentlewomen of the Bedchamber to the Queen.

Mrs. *Mary Anne Delabadie*, Dry Nurse to the Prince.

Mrs. *Judith Wilkes*, Her Majesty's Midwife.

Mrs. *Eliz. Pearce*, the Queen's Laundress

The Dutchess of *Richmond* and *Lenox*.

The Countess of *Litchfield*.

The Countess of *Marischal*.

George, Lord *Jefferies*, Lord Chancellor.

Robert, Earl of *Sunderland*.

Henry, Lord *Arundel* of *Wardour*, Lord Privy Seal.

John, Earl of *Mulgrave*, Lord Chamberlain of the Household.

William, Earl of *Craven*.

Lewis, Earl of *Feversham*, Lord Chamberlain to *Catherine*, Queen Dowager.

Alexander, Earl of *Murray*.

Charles, Earl of *Middleton*.

John, Earl of *Melfort*.

Sidney, Lord *Godolphin*, Lord Chamberlain to the Queen.

Sir *Stephen Fox*, Kt.

Lieutenant Colonel *Edward Griffin*, afterwards Lord *Griffin*.

Sir *Charles Scarborough*, Kt. First Physician to the King.

Sir *Thomas Witherly*, Second Physician to the King.

Sir *William Wald-grave*, Kt. First Phy-cian to Her Majesty.

Dr. *Robert Brady*, One of His Majesty's Physicians in ordinary.

James St. Amand, Their Majesties Apothecary.

All these declar'd, with some little Differing Circumstances, the Birth of the Prince; the greatest part, as they attested, having seen it before it was cleans'd from the Impurities of its Birth, with all other infallible Tokens of his being immediately born of the Queen's Body.

After these Depositions were taken, the King was pleas'd to acquaint the Lords, that the Princess *Anne* of *Denmark*, his Daughter, wou'd have been present, but that she being with child, and having not lately stirr'd abroad, cou'd not come so far without Hazard. *And now my Lords,* adds the *King, altho' I did not question but all here present were before satisfy'd in this Matter; yet by what you have heard, you will be the better able to satisfy others. Besides, if I and the Queen cou'd be thought so wicked as to endeavor to impose a Child upon the Nation, you see how impossible it wou'd have been; neither cou'd I my self be impos'd upon, having constantly been with the Queen, during her being with child, and the whole time of her Labour. And there is none of you but will easily believe me, who have suffer'd so much for Conscience-sake, uncapable of so great a Villany, to the Prejudice of my own Children. And I thank God, that those who know me, know well it is my Principle to do as I wou'd be done by, For that is the Law and the Prophets, And I wou'd rather dye a*

Thousand

Thousand Deaths, than do the least wrong to any of my Children.

If any of my Lords think it necessary the Queen should be sent for, it shall be done ; which the Lords declin'd, saying they had receiv'd satisfaction enough from what the King had declar'd.

Then an Order of Council was made, " That the Declarations before made, by " His Majesty, and by Her Majesty the " Queen Dowager; together with the several " Depositions then enter'd, shou'd be forth- " with enroll'd in the Court of *Chancery.*

In pursuance of which Order of Council, the Lord Chancellor, on *Saturday* the 27th of *October* following, in the High Court of *Chancery*, many of the Nobility, and the Lords of His Majesty's most Honorable Privy Council, being present, caus'd the aforesaid Order of Council, and the Declarations of His Majesty, and the Q Dowager, to be openly and distinctly read in Court, as the same were enter'd in the Words aforesaid in the Council Book And the Lords and Ladies, who made the respective Depositions aforesaid, being present in Court, were sworn again, and having heard their Depositions distinctly read in the Words aforesaid, and being severally interrogated by the Court to the Truth thereof, they all upon their Oaths affirmed their respective Depositions to be true , and did likewise depose (except some few, who came late into the Council Chamber, or some who stood at too great a distance) that they heard His Majesty, and Her Majesty the Queen Dowager, make the several Declarations aforesaid,

and

and that the same, as they had been read, were truly enter'd into the Council Book, according to the Sense, Intent, and Meaning of what His Majesty the King, and Her Majesty the Queen Dowager did then declare. And for as much as the Earl of *Huntingdon*, and the Earl of *Peterborow*, who were not able to depose the Matters aforesaid, had not been examin'd at the Council Board, but had brought their several Depositions in Writing, which they deliver'd into Court, and were to the same effect with the rest, the Lord Chancellor caus'd them to be openly read, and examin'd them severally upon their Oaths to the Truth thereof. Whereupon his Majesty's Attorney General mov'd the Court, that the said Declarations of His Majesty, and of Her Majesty the Queen Dowager; and the several Depositions, and the Order of Council, shou'd be enroll'd in the *Petty Bag Office*, and in the Office of Enrolments in the Court of *Chancery*, for the safe Preservation and Custody of them, which the Lord Chancellor order'd accordingly.

Before this His Majesty had receiv'd the Compliments of Congratulation from most of the Princes of *Europe*, the Prince and Princess of *Orange* not excepted; and Addresses from all Parts of the Kingdom to the same purpose. And not only this, but the most Sprightly and Ingenious of the Two Universities employ'd their Pens in celebrated Verses, to congratulate the King on this Occasion There seem'd a glorious Interval of Peace and Happiness, and a hopeful Promise of Lasting and Infinite Blessings to the Nation;

Nation; but in the Mazes of Providence there is something ordained for Man not to see, and which the most glorious and fair Appearance of is only delusive. In One of those famous pieces of Poetry I have mention'd, the Author seems to have had much such another *Thought*, and indeed to prophesy something of Futurity.

ONCE more my *Goddess*, hear thy *Priest*,
    Indulge me, O indulge this last *Request*!
The *Mightiest Boon* thou hast in store,
I ask, but grant, and I will ask no more.

Oh let me enter to the *Inmost Room*,
The darken'd *Retirement* of Apollo's *Doom*.
    The sacred *Mirror* there expose,
        The wondrous *Magic-Glass*,
        Which from its bright reflective *Face*,
    Fate's inmost *Secrets* shows,
        And great *Futurities* already come to pass.

There I wou'd view when James shall late repair,
    In the first Orbs to shine a *Star*;
And guide with guardian Rays, his *People* from afar.
    There I wou'd view his Godlike *Son*
With Shouts ascend his *Father's Throne*;
And cheer, with mighty Hopes, the drooping Albion.

        Next, *Goddess*, I wou'd see him reign,
        Crown'd and uncontrol'd, the *Monarch* of
                                        [the *Main*.
        Whilst humble Belgians sue for *Peace*,
        And the far *East* and *West* the British *Power confess*.

E   *Let*

Let him next on Land appear,
Bold, yet cautious, open, and yet wise,
Generous, and yet frugal, good without Disguise.
With Justice mild, and piously severe.
Shew me Goddess, shew me this,
And let thy Oracles to morrow cease.

Alas, the Muse the well meant Pray'r denies,
She struts, frowns, and thus replies ·
With Furious Folly, and with Zeal Profane,
The uneasy *Britains* still wou'd pry
Into the Depths of late Futurity ;
Whilst Heaven showers present Blessings down
[in vain.
What Time shall come, and what the Fates
[will do.
Concerns not thee, O Man, to know ;
To day is thine, O seize the useful Now !
But nothing happy, Man can please,
Wanton and lawless grown, with Luxury
[and Ease.

How near this Poet hit the Temper of his
Countrymen, I need not shew , they were not
to be pleas'd, Cabals were form'd against the
King, and an Intelligence kept with the
Prince of *Orange*, who was invited over, and
being succour'd by the *Hollanders*, appointed a
numerous Fleet, with which he pass'd into
England with an Army of 13000 Men. The
King in a very indulgent manner, offer'd
whatever his Subjects cou'd reasonably require, if Reason and their own Interest cou'd
have reclaim'd them , but the Frenzy was
grown too strong   The Prince was advancing
with his Troops, and the King seeing no other
means

means of healing this Breach, put himself at the head of his Army, and march'd against the Enemy, when drawing near to them, he soon found what he had to trust to; his Army was instantly abandon'd by almost all its Officers, most of which had been gain'd by the Prince of *Orange*'s Emissaries, who instead of doing their Duty to attack him, went over to him.

The Desertion in short was so general, that the King's own Creatures forsook him, and even those he had overwhelm'd with his Royal Goodness were found in the Confedecacy. In this Confusion of Affairs he judg'd it improper to continue at the head of such an Army, from whom he cou'd promise himself no Subjection, and therefore retired again to *London*.

Mean time provision was to be made for the Security of the Queen, and Prince of *Wales* (then so call'd) who was now not above Six Months old, whom the King caus'd privately to pass into *France*, and intended himself soon to follow them. At length he got out of *Whitehall*, parted from *London*, and imbark'd; but being oblig'd to put ashore again for Ballast, he was arrested and discover'd near *Feversham*, where he was so rudely treated by the Mob, as very much exercis'd his Royal Patience; the Dignity of his Person not being sufficient to guard him from those mean Insolencies, which but to a Private Person wou'd have been accounted infamous Outrages. Here however he receiv'd the courtesy of having his wearing Cloaths brought him, being sent on board a Man of War then in the

Hope, below *Gravesend*, for that purpose; and as soon as 'twas known at *London* of his being stopp'd at *Feversham*, the Lords sent him his Coaches and Guards, and at the same time deputed the Earl of *Feversham* to go and engage him to come back

The King had no time to deliberate, for he was no longer Master of his own Proceedings, and therefore took Coach and submitted to be conducted to *London*: The People, by their loud Acclamations, testifying an extraordinary Joy and entire Devotion to the King's Interest; which was but a Transitory Comfort, for about Midnight, when the King lay fast asleep void of all Fear and Suspicion, the Lords *Hallifax*, *De la Mere*, and *Shrewsbury*, came to awake him, and to tell him from the Prince of *Orange*, that it was found necessary for him to retire from *London*. They offer'd him at the same time his Choice of *Hampton Court* or *Ham*, for the Place of his Retreat, but the King desir'd to go to *Rochester*, which was granted him, and thither he was carry'd Prisoner.

Here he continued some few Days, always bearing in mind that he was a *Christian* and a King, till he met with a favorable Opportunity for his Escape. There was a Boat waited for him at the Sea side, the King pass'd unobserv'd thro' a Garden, stepp'd into the Boat, and set sail for *France*, whither in a Day or two he happily arriv'd He was received in *France* with all the Marks of Honor and Distinction suitable to his Character, and hasting to St. *Germans* he there found the Queen and Prince (so call'd) newly arriv'd

And

And here one may pretty well judge what were the Sentiments of the Hearts of their *Britannic* Majesties at this afflicting, yet joyful Interview. They now saw one another again after so sorrowful a Parting, and so many Dangers they had both undergone ; but at the same time cou'd not but reflect deeply on the Condition they were reduc'd to, which yet was very much alleviated by the obliging and generous Offers of the King of *France*, and the repeated Promises he made them, to succor and assist them with all his Power.

But this mutual Comfort of seeing one another again did not last long, the King had not been above Two Months at St. *Germans*, before he thought himself oblig'd, for the Good of his Affairs, to pass into *Ireland*, where the Lord *Tyrconnel*, at the head of the *Catholicks*, still maintain'd the King's Authority.   The King sail'd thither, and there sustain'd the War against Duke *Schombergh* for above a Twelvemonth, till King *William* arriving with a numerous Force of veteran Troops, had the advantage of the King's Army, and defeated him at the Passage of the *Boyne*, after which he was advised by My Lord *Tyrconnel*, and all the General Officers to retreat to *France*, where, about Two Years after, his Queen bore him a Daughter, who was born the 28th of *June*, 1691, and christen'd *Louise Marie*, about the time of her Father's Disappointment by the Defeat at *La Hogue* ; from which time the Residue of his Life was wholly employ'd in Exercises of Piety and Devotion, of which he was a very shining Example to the time of his Death.

Fo

For some time before which he made it his daily Prayer to God, that He would be pleas'd to take him out of this troublesome World, and on this Subject he had some conversation with the Queen, who seem'd very sensibly afflicted at his having so passionate a desire of Death, telling him that she look'd upon the Preservation of his Person as necessary for the Good of her and her Children. But she receiv'd no other Answer but this, *That God Almighty wou'd take care of her, and her Children, and that his Life gave him no Capacity of doing any thing for them.* He wou'd often have communication with his Children, especially the Prince of *Wales* (as they then call'd him) in whom the King was infinitely delighted, as finding in him, tho' yet very young, a Genius capable of arriving at the highest Accomplishments, which the King wou'd passionately indulge him in, and by repeated Instructions take all imaginable care to fructify his tender Mind with the most Useful and Noble Sentiments, to which in Nature he seem'd so apparently inclin'd.

About *Midsummer*, 1701, the King was seiz'd with a dead Palsy, and grew dangerously ill upon it. The Physicans being of opinion that he might receive some benefit from the Waters of *Bourbon*, he went thither, and took 'em with some Success: But some Months after he began to spit Blood again, as he had done before his Journey to *Bourbon*, and on the 2d of *September* he was taken very ill, in which State he continued for Two Days, and then his Physicians began to despair of his Life The same Day he
made

made a general Confeſſion, which he had ſcarce finiſh'd before he was taken with ſuch a Weakneſs as was follow'd by a Vomiting of Blood, which had like to have choak'd him, however, he recover'd himſelf a little, and call'd for the Prince of *Wales* (as then call'd) who immediately enter'd the Chamber; but it was a ſad Spectacle for him to ſee the King cover'd with Blood, and half dead. He ran to embrace him, and the King held out his Arms to him himſelf, and embrac'd him with all the Tenderneſs imaginable. He bleſs'd him, and as he gave him his benediction, recommended to him above all things to ſtand faſt by his Religion, and the Service of God, whatever came of it, and to have always for the Queen all the reſpect and ſubmiſſion due to the Beſt of Mothers. He likewiſe let him underſtand how much he was indebted to the King of *France*, which he charg'd him never to forget: What elſe the King had to ſay to him, he gave him in Writing, and bid him read it often when His Majeſty was gone, a Copy of which is hereafter printed.

It was not without ſome Violence that the P—— was taken from him, the King would fain have held him, *Leave me my Son*, ſaid he, *let me give him my Bleſſing once more*; which when he had done, he ſuffer'd him to retire to his own Apartment. After which the King order'd the Princeſs his Daughter to be brought him, to whom he ſpoke much in the ſame Terms, and gave her his bleſſing: And the Princeſs, melted into Tears, gave him to underſtand by the Abundance of 'em the inward Sorrow of her Heart

When

When the King had done speaking to his Children, he order'd the *Protestant* Lords, and his Domesticks of the same Religion, who were in his Chamber, to come near him. He exhorted them every one in particular to embrace the *Catholic* Religion, assuring them that if they follow'd his Advice he gave 'em, they wou'd feel the same Consolation that he did, whenever they found themselves in the same Condition they then saw him in. Nor did he forget the *Catholicks*, whom he exhorted to live according to their Faith, and all together to pay a lasting and just obedience to the P——

The King of *France*, who had not miss'd One Day to inform himself of the state of his Health, and had been already twice to see him, paid him a third visit. His *Most Christian* Majesty went first into the Queen's Chamber, where he declared to her the Resolution he had taken, That *provided it pleas'd God to take the King her Husband, he wou'd acknowledge the Prince of* Wales (as he was then call'd) *for King of* England, Upon which the Queen sent immediately for him, and acquainted him with what His *Most Christian* Majesty design'd to do in his favor; to whom the King resuming the Discourse, said, *Sir, you are going to lose the King your Father, but you shall always find another in me, and I shall look on you as my own Child* At which the P—— embracing the King's Knees, assur'd him, *That he wou'd also have the same respect for His Majesty, as he had had for the King his F——r That he wou'd never forget how much he was indebted to him, but preserve the Acknow-ledgement of it while he liv'd*

The

The King of *France* pass'd from thence into the King of *England*'s Apartment, and went to his Bedside. The Courtiers out of respect wou'd have withdrawn ; but his *Most Christian* Majesty signify'd to them, that he wou'd be glad to have the World know what he had to say ; then addressing himself to the Sick King, he repeated aloud what he had before declar'd to the Queen concerning the P——, adding withal, to the King's Consolation , *That he perceiv'd in him those early Appearances of Vertue and Honor, that could not but strengthen His Majesty in his Affection to him, besides the Obligations of Conscience and Affinity, which he had always Indispensably thought himself under.*

It is impossible to represent the Sentiments of the *English* Court upon this Occasion. Without any regard to the measures of Decency, every one was eager to testify their grateful Acknowledgements to the *Most Christian* King. They threw themselves at his Feet, and in Sentiments mingled with Comfort and Sorrow, made the Chamber ring with Applauses and Sighs, insomuch that the Thanks of His *Britannic* Majesty could not be heard : And the *Most Christian* King found himself so sensibly touch'd, that he could scarce refrain from Tears, and therefore retir'd.

I shall here repeat no more of this sad Catastrophe of the *English* King, he lay till the 16th of *September*, when he resign'd his Soul to God, and was with very Little Pomp and Ceremony interr'd in the Parish Church of St. *Germans,* as a private Gentleman, according

to

to the Request of his Will, and no Epitaph on his Tomb, but these four words, *Here lies King* James.

Thus I have run thro' the Life of this unfortunate King, which I shall conclude with the Instructions he left in Writing to the Prince of *Wales*, as he was then call'd ; but penn'd some time before his Death.

KINGS *not being responsable for their Actions, but to God only, they ought to behave themselves in every thing with more Circumspection than those that are of an Inferior Condition ; and if Subjects owe a faithful Obedience to their King, and his Laws, the King is likewise obliged to take a great care of 'em, and to love them like a Father. Then as you hold the first rank among 'em, and that you must be one day their King your self, I believe it to be my Duty, as your King, and your Father, to give you the following advice : And I find my self yet more obliged to it, when I reflect on your Age, my own, and the present State of my Affairs.*

I. Serve *Ged* as a perfect Christian, *and be a worthy Child of the* Roman Church. *Let no Humane Consideration, of what nature soever, be ever capable to draw you from it. Remember always that Kings and Princes, and the Great Ones of the Earth, shall give an account of their Conduct before the Dreadful Tribunal of God, where every one shall be judged according to his Works. Consider that you are come into the World to glorify God and not to seek your Pleasure. That it is by Him that Kings reign , and that without His particular Protection, nothing can prosper of all what you un-*
dertake

dertake. Serve then the Lord in the Days of your
Youth, and you shall receive a Recompence in the
Land of the Living. Begin by times, and without Delay. Never forget that there are greater
things expected from Persons in High Stations, than
from others: Their Example gives great impressions, and is always most follow'd, be it as it will.

II If it pleases God to re-establish me upon my
Throne, I have reason to hope that I shall put
things in that Condition, that it shall be more ea-
sy for you to govern my Kingdoms after me, with
Security of the Monarchy, and intire Satisfaction
of all the Subjects. A King cannot be happy if
his Subjects be not at ease, and the Subjects also
cannot securely enjoy what belongs to them if their
King be not at his ease, and in a capacity to pro-
tect and defend them. Therefore preserve your
Prerogatives, but disquiet not your Subjects, either in their Estates or their Religion. Remember the great Precept, Do not to others what you
would not have done to your self. Take great care
that no body oppresses the People with Vexatious
Law-Suits, or Undertakings that are chargeable to
them I told you, and it is true, that a King
ought to be the Father of his People, and conse-
quently to have a tenderness for 'em that is altogether fatherly.

III Live in peace with your Neighbors, and
know that Kings and Princes may commit the
same Injustice with the most notorious Robbers,
that openly attack the Passengers upon the High-
Ways, or the Pyrates, that take whatever they
meet Without doubt they'll be punish'd for it at
the Judgment of God. Then suffer your self not to

be

be drawn away by *Ambition*, and the *Desire* of *a*
False Glory, so far as to forget the *Precept* of *the*
Law of *God* and *Nature*, which I told you *but*
just now. *Hearken* not to the *Counsels* of *those*
that shall persuade you to enlarge your *Estates* and
Dominions by *Unjust Acquisitions*, but be *content*
with what is your own.

IV. *Do* your endeavor to establish by a *Law*
the *Liberty* of *Conscience*; and whatever may *be*
represented to you about it, never leave that *De-*
sign until you have compass'd it. It is a grace *and*
particular favor that *God* does them, whom *He*
enlightens with *His Knowledge*, in calling them *to*
the *True Religion*, and it is by *Mildness*, *Instru-*
ctions, and a good *Example*, that they are *won*
much more than by *Fear* or *Violence*.

V. *If* you begin early to live well, it will *be*
much easier to you to preserve your *Innocence*, *than*
to recover it after once you shall have lost *it*
Forget not the good *Instructions* that have been *gi-*
ven you, to shun *Idleness*, and *Bad Company*
Idleness will expose you to all sorts of *Temptation*
and *Bad Company* will be a *Poison* to you, of *which*
you'll hardly scape the *Influences* *Suffer* no *Per-*
sons to come near you that talk obscenely or *im-*
piously, and by their *Railleries* endeavor to destroy
Christianity it self, and turn into ridicule *the*
most *Holy* and *Religious Practices*.

VI *Nothing* is more fatal to *Men*, and to *the*
Greatest Men (I speak with a dear-bought *Expe-*
rience) than to be given over to the *Unlawful*
Love of *Women*, which of all *Vices* is the most *se-*
ducing, and the most difficult to be conquer'd, *if*
not

not stifled in its Birth: It is a Vice that is but too universal and too common in Young People; there are but few that apply themselves to know the Danger of it, and are not drawn to it by Bad Example, as well as the Suggestions and Artifices of the Devil; no body ought to be so much upon his guard as your self; because it has pleased God to make you, by your Birth, what you are, for the more Men are elevated, the more they are exposed; especially if they live in Peace and Plenty. But what ought more to oblige you to watch over your self, is the Remembrance of the terrible Example of David, he was hardly establish'd in his Throne, but he forgot the great things that God had done for him, and suffer'd his Eyes to be dazled by the Sight of a Woman, so far as to fall into the Sin of Adultery, and from Adultery into that of Murder. Could but all, that, with him, have had the misfortune of falling into those heinous Crimes, remember the sincere Repentance he had of 'em, and imitate him; not forgetting the Chastisements and Afflictions that God sent him in this World, to save him in the next.

VII. Master your self so much as never to be transported by Anger. That Passion offends God, and is grating to Men, and while it lasts, takes away the Reason and Judgment of him that gives himself over to it. It has been the Ruin of several Great Men. What a King says is not easily forgot, and there is nothing but Fear and Religion that can hinder Men from resenting it, and being revenged of it Anger makes a Prince incapable of governing, for how shall he rule others, that cannot rule himself.

VIII.

VIII. Take not pleasure in feasting ; but shun all sorts of Excesses that ruin Health, and makes Men unfit for Business. It is very hard to leave the Habit of 'em when once it is contracted. The Excess of Wine kills in a short time those that are of a Hot Constitution, and besots them that are Phlegmatic. I believe it is not necessary to enlarge upon this Point, since few Princes among the Civiliz'd Nations are addicted to so foul a Vice.

IX. I must yet give you warning not to suffer your self to be engaged, either by the Heat of Youth, Ambition, Interest, or flattering Councils, into an Offensive War that is not evidently just : Otherwise it would be all at once to violate the divine and humane Laws. Kings and Princes, to come again to the Comparison which I made you, can no more justify the Injustice which they do to their Neighbors, in taking (unless it be by way of Reprisal) their Cities and Provinces, than the Highway-men and Pirates can that which they do to Private Persons, when forcibly they take away their Goods. You ought, when Necessity requires it, to preserve and defend what is lawfully your own, in taking up Arms, and repelling Force by Force. You owe that to your self, you owe it to your Subjects. But to be the Aggressor in an Unjust War, is an Undertaking of Fatal Consequence for this Life, and that to come For in the first place, God pardons not, if we make not restitution. And that Princes seldom do. In the second place, what Devastation makes not War in Provinces and whole Kingdoms, by the Ruin of so many Thousands of innocent Persons? Besides these general Rules of Conscience, a King of England ought of good Politicks to be more circumspect in this Point, than

any

any other. For not being able, without the Assistance of his People, to begin and carry on a War, and the People of England never believing it their Interest to furnish Money for making conquests abroad, it follows necessarily, that the Charges of the War fall upon the King's Funds, and upon what we call the CIVIL LIST, and that so the King gets in debt.

X. For the same reason a King of England ought to take care that in his Expences he exceeds not his Revenue, and that he applies himself to what is agreeable to the People, and tends to the Public Good. If you find any of your Ministers, or Officers, that abusing the Power which you have trusted 'em with, employ it to vex and oppress your Subjects, take away their Places, and punish 'em your self, without giving 'em over to the Examination of a Parliament, who desire no better than to snatch 'em out of your hands, and bring 'em to justice themselves; which would but weaken your Authority, and discourage those that serve you faithfully.

XI. Apply your self principally to know the Constitution of the English Government, that you may keep, both you and your Parliament, each in the due Bounds that become the one and the other. Further, be instructed concerning the Trade of the Nation, make it flourish by all Lawful Means. It is that which enriches the Kingdom, and which will make you considerable abroad. But above all, endeavor to be and to remain superior at Sea, without which England cannot be secure.

The

The Prince (as he was then call'd) was about Thirteen Years of Age at the Death of King *James*, fraught with the blooming Appearance of all manly Virtues, which now began to ripen in him, so as to attract the eyes of the Court of *France*. 'Tis true, the King's generous Design of declaring him King of *England*, according to the Promise he had given, did not pass uninterrupted thro' the Council, yet even those who disapprov'd it, took pride in excusing themselves from any manner of Prejudice and Disrespect, but on the contrary declar'd, " They shou'd be " glad of any Opportunity to serve him, " whose Interest they cou'd never think of " deserting, were not that of their own " Country in the Scale, the inevitable Com- " mencement of a War depending from the " express Terms of a Peace very lately con- " cluded. And therefore if they did not " think this a proper Season to proclaim his " Title, they cou'd not doubt but they shou'd " merit His Majesty's, and the P——'s Ex- " cuse in what they had said. The D—— *de T*——, the D—— *de M*——, the Counts of *V*—*e, d*— *C*——, M. *Ch—d*, and others, were of this opinion, but the King was stedfast in his Resolution, and the Dauphin, who was the last that spoke in Council, left no Objection unanswer'd, either in respect to the King's Honor or Advantage, that did not entirely convince His Majesty of the Justice and Integrity of such a Proceeding, and of the same opinion were all the Princes of the Blood

The

The King, who in his Heart was refolv'd before, took a great deal of Pleafure in the *Dauphine*'s Words, and immediately gave Orders for the proclaiming him King of *Great Britain*, &c. as foon as the Breath was out of King *James*'s Body, and the People very willingly proclaim'd their Satisfaction, by joining in it their loud and hearty Acclamations. The ufual Ceremony on this Occafion being punctually obferv'd: The Queen Mother was appointed Regent, my Lord *Middleton* gave up the Seal, all the Lords took the Oaths of Fidelity, the Servants kifs'd his Hand, and every thing ftood as it did in King *James*'s Days.

The King of *France*, (who had not only Proclaim'd him in his own Dominions, but had likewife given Orders to his Embaffadors to do the fame in all the Courts of *Europe*) thought it now a very great Argument of his Affection to him, to take care of his future Education · Thus far he had proceeded in all neceffary Literature, and was ready to be initiated in the more Manly Exercifes of Life: His moft Chriftian Majefty therefore order'd him proper Mafters at his own Expence; to inftruct him in the moft ufeful parts of the Mathematicks, particularly Navigation, Fortification, and the like; the former of which (Navigation) he is faid to be an exquifite Mafter of, as he is likewife of moft of the European Languages. To thefe more Mafculine Accomplifhments were added Riding, Dancing, Fencing, Shooting, and fuch like Embellifhments, as together make up the

Character

Character of the Perfon that the *French* had
proclaim'd him to be.

Thofe who have convers'd with him, al-
low him to be Endu'd with excellent Wit,
and thofe who have feen him under the
Trials of it, are of the fame Opinion as to
his Courage. In the Twelfth Year of his
Age, as he was Hunting with the Duke of
Berry and others in the Foreft of St *Germain*
they had a monftrous Boar in Chafe, the
Company were difpers'd and the (pretended
Prince meeting the Boar feparately, having
only with him one Servant, fhot him in the
Body and ended the Purfuit. At which kind
of Exercifes of Shooting Running, or Flying
there are few among the *French*, tho' the
are very Excellent at it, that exceed him
His Dexterity in Riding and Fencing migh
likewife be added among thefe other Qual
fications, but it is enough to fay, that ther
was nothing wanting to contribute any thin
to his Education. Thus far the Accounts (
French Authors go He is proclaim'd ther
and ftil'd King of *England*, a Detachment (
Fifty of the French Guards appointed hir
with Twelve Yeoman of the Guard, S
Guard du Corps, a proper Divifion
Houfhold Servants, and an Allowance
50000 Livres a Month, convey'd conftant
to St *Germains* in an Iron Cart; togeth
with a *Private-Purfe* from the *French* Cou
of near as much more· And here we lea
him a little to fee how this is relifh'd
other Places.

In *England*, the People seem'd to be in a wonderful Suprize. For they had been taught to look on him as an Impostor, and his most Christian Majesty had, to reap the Fruits of Peace, but a little before acknowledg'd King *William*, as King of *Great Britain*, who being a Prince of a very great Spirit, was sufficiently rouz'd by such a Proceeding. He immediately writ to the King of *Sweden*, as Guarantee of the Treaty of *Ryswick*, to give him an Account of the manifest Violation thereof, and at the same time sent an Express to the Earl of *Manchester*, his Embassador at *Paris*, to come immediately away, without taking leave; and Monsieur *Poussin*, the *French* Secretary here had suddain Notice to depart the Kingdom, The Nation address'd the King, and agreed in an unanimous Adherence to his Majesty, expressing an Abhorrence of this Action in the *French* King, so that many who were no Enemies to the Person proclaim'd, began to fear his most Christian Majesty had proceeded a Step too far.

King *William* was so Active, that he immediately form'd the Grand Alliance, which the *French* were not able to prevent, and then Dissolving the Parliament, call'd a new One, before whom he laid the Copies of those Treaties, which they unanimously approv'd; and one of the first Things transacted, was the passing an Act for the Attainder of the (Pretended) Prince of *Wales*. But this was hardly done before King *William* died; Yet Matters were so far carried in Parliament, that a War was inevitable, which had been

already

already begun in *Italy*, and of which I have not room here to repeat any thing, if it were material, more than saying, that the *French* King meerly drew it on himself thro' his immoveable and generous Principle of supporting the (Pretended) Prince; for he might otherwise have made very good Terms for his Grandson, by a reasonable Partition, or at least have warded off the *English* share in it, which has been much the heaviest, and without which, this War cou'd not in humane Probability, but have prov'd successful on his side.

On the contrary, in the Year 1706. The most Christian King found himself under the Necessity of suing for Peace; yet it was not without severe Struggles of Conscience to depart from the Promises he had made the late King *James* II. He consulted the Court of St. *Germains*, and in a private Conference with the Queen Dowager, and the (preten ted) Prince at that time, " assur'd them that " he wou'd never depart from their Interest " tho' the present Exigency of Affairs, and " the pressing Instances of his Subjects had " oblig'd him to make some Overtures o " Peace to the Enemy. They return'd hi " Majesty's Compliment with Sighs; and ' the (pretended) Prince himself replied ' That not only his Interest, but even hi " Life it self, was too small a Consideratio " for his most Christian Majesty to put i " Composition with the Good of his King " dom. *I am content*, says he, *to leave m Cause to Providence, being entirely assur'd o your Majesty's sincere Affection to me.*

How

However, for the prefent, his Majefty's good Wifhes for Peace were baffled, by fome who thought it their Intereft to carry on the War, and wou'd be contented with nothing but the utter Ruin of the *French* Nation, which when the King found, he exerted himfelf in a very wonderful Manner, the Offers of Peace that he had made, foftned the Hearts of his Subjects, and very much help'd to alleviate the Hardfhips they lay under, fo that his Majefty, contrary to the Expectations of the Enemy, and even furpaffing their Belief, was in a Capacity next Year, not only to ftop the Torrent of the Confederates in *Flanders*, but to be Victorious in *Spain*, at the Battle of *Almanza*. In *Germany* the Marfhal *de Villars* likewife made a very advantageous Irruption into *Germany*; and in *Provence* the Allies had been forc'd to Retreat from before *Toulon*. As thefe Succeffes did not a little Elevate the drooping Spirits of the *French* Nation, fo it likewife put fome Life into the Court of St. *Germains*.

Another thing was likewife before the *French* Court, that promis'd them fome Advantage. The *Scotch* Lords at St. *Germains*, had not been idle, in improving the Opportunity the Union of the two Kingdoms had given them to found the Depth of the Male-contented Party in *Scotland*; and fo good a Correfpondence was held there, that they had the earlieft Notice of all that pafs'd, and how the Nation ftood affected, which was conftantly communicated at *Verfailles*. The *French* King, however, with his ufual Caution, was not too hafty to credit the Bufinefs, tho' it appear'd

to have a very good face, till a List was produc'd to him of the Names of many Leading
Men in *Scotland* that were ready to receive
(as they call'd it) their lawful King *James*
VIII. The King therefore, at the repeated
inftances of the *Scotch* Lords, difpatch'd thither the *Marquis de Nangis*, by whom he fent
the neceffary Arms for an Expedition, and order'd him to bring back the beft Intelligence
poffible, not only of the Truth of what had
been laid before him, but what Force wou'd
be requir'd to put it in action, and what
Strength the *English* wou'd be able to fend
thither on a fudden; who upon his Return
brought the King large Affurances of having
a ftrong Party in that Kingdom ready to join
them, and all manner of reafonable Hopes of
fucceeding in the Enterprize.

Under thefe Circumftances, the Affair was
difpatch'd to the Court of *Rome*, and related
with fuch feeling Aggravation of being a great
Means towards promoting the Caufe of the
Holy *Catholic* Religion; and likewife fo tenderly remonftrated by the (pretended)
Prince himfelf in a dutiful and moving Letter
to His Holinefs, that he was prevail'd with
to furnifh a confiderable Sum of Money toward fo hopeful an Expedition, which he re-
mitted to *France*. And fo diligent was His
Aloft Chriftian Majefty in expending it in the
neceffary Preparations for this Expedition,
which were tranfacted with fuch Secrecy,
that the Defign was rather guefs'd at than
known, and every thing got ready before the
Spring.

The

The *Chevalier De St. George* (for this was the Name he had now assum'd) who had had several Interviews with the *French* King on this Occasion, was charm'd with this new Opportunity of putting himself into the World, having a secret Impulse of Glory that spurr'd him forwards to appear in something worthy of the Character that was given him; and of putting in action those Rudiments of Honor, which he had learn'd with so much Pleasure. He now receiv'd the compliments of the Chief of the *French* Nobility on his intended Expedition, who flock'd to wish him good success therein: and he likewise in his turn visited the Princes and Princesses of the Blood, and if we may believe Report (for it will be no Wonder to find Love in the Breast of a sanguine P—— at the Age of 20) he paid something more than a formal visit of leave to the blooming *Madmoiselle de C——*, on whom he had look'd for some time with such passionate eyes, as made it whisper'd at Court, that they too apparently betray'd something more than a common Respect due to so celebrated a Beauty. Why this Affair has been no more talk'd of, is perhaps the Reasons of State that moved in the Necessity of dissipating such a Match; and tho' of late, thro' the prevailing Persuasions of the Queen, it has been less a Subject of Discourse at Court, yet 'tis certain he never speaks of her to this Day without discovering the tender Remains of a broken and disappointed Passion.

To return therefore to his Military Affairs; the day before his Departure from *St. Germans*, the K. of *France* came thither to pay him a visit fit, and bid him adieu. He receiv'd the King in the moſt dutiful and affectionate manner, having a great Crowd of Courtiers about him, and began with expreſſing ſome extraordinary Sentiments of Thanks for what the King had been pleas'd to do for him in this Affair. The King told him very gayly, that he came not to receive his thanks for it, but to wiſh him good ſucceſs, and likewiſe to furniſh him with a Sword, which he deſired him to wear in the Cauſe he went on, and to remember if it prov'd ſucceſsful that it was a *French* Sword. The Chevalier return'd the Compliment, by aſſuring His *Moſt Chriſtian* Majeſty, " That " if it were his good fortune to get poſſeſſion " of the Throne of his Anceſtors, he wou'd " not content himſelf with returning him " Thanks by Letters and Embaſſadors, but " wou'd ſhew his Gratitude by his Actions. The King likewiſe ask'd him if he was ſatisfy'd in the choice of Officers and Servants that he had made to attend him? To which the *Chevalier* reply'd, That, as in every thing elſe, ſo even in that, he left it entirely at His Majeſty's Diſpoſal.

And now having taken his final leave, he ſet out for *Dunkirk* on the 8th of *March* (N. S.) Nor will it be neceſſary to reiterate the ſad Parting between him and the Queen; as likewiſe the Princeſs his (ſuppos'd) Siſter. The Grief of the former was inexpreſſible, unleſs thro' the Multitude of Tears which ſhe ſhed, that cou'd beſt delineate it; ſhe embrac'd him often, and ſunk under a thouſand Fears and Cares for his Safety, as if ſhe ſeem'd to doubt of ever ſeeing him again: The latter likewise drown'd in Tears, hung about him in a very tender and affectionate Manner, and Expref's'd very dreadful Apprehenfions fhe conceiv'd of his Safety.

In the mean time, while every-thing was hurrying on for that Expedition; the *French* King who had entertain'd great Hopes of it's Succef's, thought it no longer worthy to be made a Secret, and therefore fent the following Circular Letter to his Minifters at *Rome, Switzerland,* and *Geneva,* and other Neuteral Places, the very next Day after the Chevalier's Departure.

" I Have long been of Opinion, that the " affifting the King of *England* to poffef's the " Throne of his Anceftors, wou'd be for " the general Good of *Europe*; I believe that " a Peace wou'd be the Confequence of it's " Succef's, and that this Prince's Subjects " will efteem themfelves equally happy to " Re-eftablifh him in the Place of his Pre- " deceffors, and in being themfelves deli- " ver'd from the continual Impofitions, " wherewith they are Over-whelm'd, *to* " maintain a War altogether Foreign to " them.

" As the *Scots* have yet more Reafon than " the *Englifh* to be Disfatisfy'd with the " prefent Government of *England*, it appears " to me a convenient Opportunity to reftore " that Nation their Lawful Sovereign, and " to enable the Prince to deliver it from the " Oppreffion it has fuffer'd fince the Revo- " lution, which happen'd under the late " King of *England* James II.

H " Thefe

" These are Reasons which have deter-
" min'd me to Equip a Squadron of my
" Ships at *Dunkirk*, and to furnish the King
" of *England* with a confiderable Number of
" my Troops, to accompany him to *Scotland*
" to fupport thofe his faithful Subjects, who
" fhall Declare for him.

" He left this Place Yefterday, to go to
" *Dunkirk*, in order to Embark and get with
" all Expedition to *Scotland*. His Intention
" is not to enter the Kingdom by Right of
" Conqueft, but to oblige them to receive
" him as Legal Poffeffor of it. He will be-
" have himfelf in like manner with Refpect
" to all his Dominions, who fhall pay the
" Obedience they owe him, and his Subjects
" will only be diftinguifh'd according to the
" Zeal and Affection they fhew for him,
" without Examining what Religion they
" profefs'd in which he leaves them to their
" entire Liberty.

" I have not Thoughts of enlarging my
" Power by affifting to Re-eftablifh this
" Prince. 'Tis fufficient that I do an Act of
" Juftice in Vindicating the Honour of
" Crown'd Heads, highly Affronted in the
" Perfon of the King his Father; and my
" Wifhes will be entirely accomplifh'd, if by
" God's Bleffing on the Endeavors, the Suc-
" cefs become the Means of procuring a la-
" fting Peace, fo neceffary to all *Europe*.

" As this Refolution of mine will foon
" fpread it felf thro' *Europe*, my Will is, that
" you fpeak of it in the Manner I Direct
" you. Given at *Verfailles* this Eighth of
" *March*, 1708.

H

His Holineſs upon this appointed public Prayers for Forty Hours, in the *Engliſh*, *Scotch*, and *Iriſh* Churches at *Rome*, for the Succeſs of the Undertaking, and granted Indulgences to ſuch as ſhou'd put up thoſe Prayers.

The *Chevalier*, upon his arrival at *Dunkirk*, found freſh Marks of the *French* King's Eſteem. He was furniſh'd with very Fine Tents, a conſiderable Quantity of Gold and Silver Houſhold Plate, of curious workmanſhip; Cloaths for his Life-Guards, Liveries for his Houſhold, and all other Neceſſaries for his Expedition. The Motto's or Devices on his Colors and Standards were adapted to the Purpoſe. On ſome there was that of the Royal Standard of *England*— *Dieu et mon Droit*, *God and my Right* : On others, *Nil deſperandum* Chriſto *Duce & Auſpice* Chriſto, *I don't deſpair ſince* Chriſt *is my Guide and Helper*. And on others, *Cui Venti & Mare obediunt, impera Domine, & fac Tranquilitatem!* O Thou *Whom the Winds and Sea obey, command Lord, that it be calm.* Whilſt he is here, waiting only the favorable Event of Wind and Weather, let us ſee what is doing elſewhere.

Notwithſtanding the great Secrecy with which this Expedition had been Concerted, it cou'd not be ſuppos'd but that Time wou'd bring about the Diſcovery of it. It was at firſt ſuſpected in *Holland*, who gave intimation to Her Majeſty's Miniſter, M. *Cadogan*. This Gentleman had a watchful Eye on theſe Preparations, but it was not till the *Chevalier* came to *Dunkirk* that he made any real Diſcovery (nor even then as to the Place

where

where they were defign'd) at what time he fent immediate notice to *England*, where on the 4th of *March* (O. S) Mr Secretary *Boyle* acquainted the Houfe of Commons, That Her Majefty had order'd him to lay before them feveral Advices receiv'd the Night before. and that Morning, of great Prepations that were making at *Dunkirk*, for an Invafion upon *England* by the *Freneh*, and that the (pretended) P. of *Wales* was come to *Dunkirk*. Which produc'd the following Addrefs to Her Majefty.

" WE Your Majefty's moft faithful and
" obedient Subjects, the Lords
" Spiritual and Temporal, and Commons of
" *Great Britain* in Parliament affembled,
" do beg leave to return our moft hearty
" Thanks to Your Majefty, for being gene-
" roufly pleafed to communicate to your
" your Parliament the Intelligence you have
" receiv'd of an intended Invafion of this
" Kingdom by the pretended Prince of
" *Wales*, fupported by a *French* Power.
" We are fo fenfible of the Happinefs we
" enjoy under Your Majefty, and are fo af-
" flicted with the dangerous Confequences of
" fuch an Attempt both to your Perfon and
" Government, that with Hearts full of
" Concern for Your Majefty's Safety, we be-
" feech Your Majefty that you will be pleafed
" to take particular care of your Royal Per-
" fon, and we on our parts are fully and una-
" nimoufly refolved to ftand by and affift Your
" Majefty with our Lives and Fortunes, in
" maintenance of your undoubted Right and
" Title

" Title to the Crown of these Realms
" against the pretended Prince of *Wales*, and
" all other your Enemies both at home and
" abroad.

" The care Your Majesty has taken for the
" defence of your Dominions, and particu-
" larly in fitting out so great a Fleet in so
" short a time, gives satisfaction and encou-
" ragement to all your Good Subjects who
" are likewise very sensible of the Zeal the
" *States General* have shewn upon this Occa-
" sion.

" As a farther Instance of our Duty we
" humbly desire that you would be pleased to
" order that the Laws against *Papists* and
" *Non-jurors* be put in Execution, and that
" directions be given to seize and secure such
" Persons, with their Horses and Arms, as
" Your Majesty shall have cause to suspect are
" disaffected to your Person and Govern-
" ment.

" And as we doubt not but by the Blessing
" of God, upon the Continuance of Your
" Majesty's Care, your Enemies will be put to
" Confusion, so we readily embrace this Op-
" portunity to shew to Your Majesty and the
" whole World, that no Attempts of this
" kind shall deter us from supporting Your
" Majesty in a vigorous Prosecution of the
" present War against *France*, till the Mo-
" narchy of *Spain* be restored to the House of
" *Austria*, and Your Majesty have the Glory
" to compleat the Recovery of the Liberties
" of *Europe*.

" *My*

My Lords, and Gentlemen.

" I Have such entire Dependance on the
" Providence of God, and so much Trust
" in the faithful Services of my good Subjects,
" that I hope this Attempt will prove Dan-
" gerous only to those who undertake it.

" I am extreamly Sensible of your Concern
" and Affection for me and my Government,
" and shall have a very particular Regard to
" the Advice you give me upon this Occa-
" sion.

" I am also very well pleas'd with the Ju-
" stice which you have done the *States General*
" in taking Notice of their timely Care for
" our Safety, and their Readiness to give
" us all possible Assistance.

" The firm Resolutions which you Ex-
" press upon all Occasions, of Supporting
" me in bringing this War to a Safe and
" Happy Conclusion, as it is most essentially
" obliging to me, so I assure my self it wil
" mightily Dishearten our Common Ene-
" mies, and give the greatest Encouragement
" and Advantage to all our Allies.

The Commons likewise order'd a Bill to be
brought in, to empower her Majesty to secure
and detain such Persons as her Majesty should
suspect were Conspiring against her Person
and Government. And pursuant to the
Parliaments Desire in their Address, a Proclamation was Issued, Declaring the *Chevalier*
and all his Accomplices, Adherents, and A-
bettors to be Traitors and Rebels. Strictly
Charging all Papist Recusants, to repair to
their

their Places of Abode, and not remove from thence above the Distance of Five Miles; and also to depart out of the Cities of *London* and *Westminster*, and from all Places within Ten Miles distance of the same.

And here it is certain, that the Catholicks in *England* and *Scotland* in many Places were great Sufferers thro' this Expedition: Who tho' they are by Principle oblig'd to wish the *Chevalier* well, yet it is thought that many of them were not over warm in this Affair, as believing if it was Unsuccessful, it wou'd be a means of laying them under fresh Hardships.

A Bill was likewise actually brought in, and ready to pass, wherein there was a Clause, for discharging Vassals from their Allegiance to their Superiors, the Leaders or Chieftains of Clans, in Case they resisted them that took part with the *Chevalier*. Besides the former united Address of the Lords and Commons, there were two other presented on the 13th of *March*, in Answer to Her Majesty's Speech of the 10th, wherein were contain'd very warm Expressions against the *Chevalier* and his Adherents.

Upon the first Notice of the *French* Armament at *Dunkirk*, Major General *Cadogan* had repaired to *Brussels*, and Concerted with Monsieur *de Auverquerque*, the March of the *British* Forces to be Shipp'd of for *Great Britain*, and how to supply their Room in their several Garrisons. From *Brussels* the Major General went to *Ghent*, and having Conferr'd with General *Lumly* the Governor of that Place, and Commander in Chief of the *British* Troops,

Troops, Orders were given to Ten Battallions to hold themfelves in a readinefs to
March at an Hours Warning. This done,
that General repaired to *Oftend*, to forward
the Preparations which were making there
for the Embarking of thofe Regiments, as
foon as there fhou'd be certain Advice, that
the Twelve *French* Battallions that were to
attend the *Chevalier* in his intended Expedition were actually Embark'd. On the other
Hand, the Admiralty of *Great Britain* fitted
out a Fleet with fuch incredible Diligence and
Expedition, that appearing in fight of *Dunkirk* before it cou'd have been expected, a
Stop was put to the Embarkation of the
Troops, and frequent Expreffes Difpatch'd
to *Paris* for new Orders. The Count *de
Fourbin* who Commanded the Squadron, having reprefented to the *French* King, That
he might indeed get out of *Dunkirk* Harbour,
and perhaps Land the Troops, but that he
cou'd not be anfwerable for his Majefty's
Ships. Notwithftanding which, he receiv'd
pofitive Inftructions to Re-imbark the Troops,
and put to Sea with the firft fair Wind.
In the mean time, to cover the Reafon of
Dis-imbarking the Troops, it was given out
that the *Chevalier* was indifpos'd of the
Meafles, attended with an Ague; but the
laft Orders coming, that pretence vanifh'd.
And Count *de Fourbin* having receiv'd Advice
that the *Britifh* Fleet, forc'd from their Station by the high Winds, was feen off the
Coaft of *Bretany*, they began to Re-imbark
the Troops, and the Wind turning fair on
the 17th of *March*, they laid hold of that

Oppor-

Opportunity, and fail'd out of *Flemifh Road*; but the Wind veering towards Night, forc'd them to anchor again in *Newport Pits*, where they continued till the 12th, and then fail'd directly for *Scotland*.

In the mean time the *Britifh* Fleet, under Sir *George Bing*, which was confiderably reinforc'd, returning to their Station off of *Graveling*, the next day receiv'd notice that the *French* Fleet was fail'd, when leaving Admiral *Baker* with a ftrong Squadron, to convoy the Troops, they fail'd directly after them to *Scotland*. Befides Ten Battallions embark'd at *Oftend*, a confiderable Reinforcement was fent from *England* toward *Scotland*, confifting of Two Troops of Guards, the Duke of *Norhumberland*'s Regiment of Horfe, a Squadron of Horfe Grenadiers, Two Regiments of Dragoons, One Detachment of 16 Men *per* Company out of the Foot Guards, befides feveral Regiments of Foot; whom the Earl of *Leven*, before difpatch'd to *Edinburgh*, was to command.

On board the *French* Ships there was 10 Battallions (befides fome Troops that were to follow them) with fufficient Stores, and 400 Non-commiffion'd Officers, for the raifing of more Forces: The whole commanded by the Count *de Gace*, a Marefchal of *France*. The *Chevalier* himfelf was on board the *Mars*, with the faid Marefchal *de Gace*, the Duke of *Perth*, the Lord *Middleton*, the Lord *Galmoy*; and other Officers, and Perfons of Diftinction. Notwithftanding the Defign was given out to be on *Scotland* in general, yet the Caftle of *Edinburgh* was the particular Place aim'd at, the

I   Plan

Plan of which had been laid before the Counci
at *Versailles*, where the Defign was unanimoufl
approv'd.

In *Scotland* at this time they were in th
greateft Confufion; thofe who were Friends u
the *Chevalier*, and wifh'd well to the Expedi
tion, were under various Apprehenfions, an
not without Fears of being feiz'd and impri
fon'd, as it happen'd to a great many; othe
were in as great Pain, not only from their A
prehenfions of the *French* Fleet, which was
invade them, but likewife of the *Chevalier*
Friends within, whom they expected to rife
arms in many Places of the Kingdom, whi
Fleet appear'd on the Coaft, having reach
the *Frith* of *Edinburgh* the 23d of *Mar*
(N S) in the Morning.

Upon Sight whereof the Country was in
alarm. At *Edinburgh* the Magiftrates affen
bled the Corporations, to know what affiftan
they cou'd expect from them in defendi
themfelves, and keeping the Peace of the (
ty? Upon which it was refolv'd that the Fr
men fhould keep guard by turns in their ref
ctive Halls, and be ready upon the firft No
of any Diforder.

On the other hand great Diligence was u
in obferving and fecuring feveral Perfons,
pected either of holding correfpondence w
the *Chevalier*, or at leaft of being inclin'c
favour his Defign; amongft whom were
Dukes of *Hamilton*, *Athol*, and *Gordon*,
many other Perfons of Note. As to
French Fleet, tho' they had been on the C
a whole Day and Night, yet no body cam
to them, and the *Englifh* follow'd then

clofe, as wholly difappointed their Landing,
and obliged them to fteer out of the *Frith*,
where they were at anchor, and to make ufe of
the Favor of the Night and a fmall Breeze, to
further their Efcape. Of which the following
Account was given by the Count *de Gace*,
otherwife call'd the Marefchal *de Mantignon*, to
M. *Chamillard*.

" SIR,

" I Had the honor to acquaint you with our
" Embarkation at *Dunkirk*, the 17th
" paft, and you fhall fee by the following
" Journal what has happen'd fince till our
" Return.
" The 17th of *March*, at 4 in the After-
" noon, the *Chevalier de Fourbin* fet fail with
" the Fleet; but about 10 in the Evening the
" Wind proving contrary, we were obliged to
" caft Anchor in the Downs of *Newport*,
" where we were detained the 18th and 19th.
" The *Proteus*, on board of which were 400
" Landmen, the *Guerrier* (or *Warrior*) and
" the *Barrentin* with 200 Men each, were
" oblig'd by the high Winds to put back into
" *Dunkirk*. The fame Day (19th) at Ten in the
" Evening, the Wind having chopped about,
" we fet fail again, and having purfu'd our
" courfe the 20th, 21ft, and 22d, with a
" ftrong Gale, we made the *Frith* of *Edin-*
" *burgh* the 23d in the Morning, and in the
" Evening caft anchor at the Mouth of it.
" The 24th in the Morning as we made ready
" to enter the *Frith*, we difcover'd a great
" Number of Ships which we foon found to be

I 2 the

" the Enemies Squadron, to the Number of
" Twenty Eight Sail, who we Judg'd to be
" the fame that appear'd off *Dunkirk*, where-
" upon Mounfieur *de Fourbin* refolv'd to bear
" off by the Favour of a Land Breeze, which
" very luckily carry'd us from the Enemy;
" The latter purfuing us very clofe all that
" Day (24) and four of their beft Sailors be-
" ing come up with our Sternmoft Ships, the
" Enemy's foremoft Ship attack'd at four in
" the Afternoon, the *Auguft* with whom fhe
" Exchanged fome Shot, for fome time after
" the *Englifh* bore down upon the *Salisbury*,
" which was more a Stern, and Endeavour'd
" to put her between her Self and another
" *Englifh* Ship that was coming up to her.
" The Fight between thofe two Ships and fome
" others on both fides lafted till Night, during
" which time, the *Salisbury* made a great Fire
" with their fmall Arms.

" Our Fleet being difpers'd, and the Ene-
" my near us, Monfieur *de Fourbin* fteer'd falfe
" during the Night, which had a good Effect,
" for the next Day (the 25th) we found our
" felves with twenty Sail at a confiderable
" Diftance from the Enemy, whereupon I
" Difcours'd Monfieur *Fourbin*, to know of
" him, whether having mifs'd our Landing in
" the *Frith* of *Edinburgh* we might not attempt
" it in another Place; He propos'd to me *In-*
" *vernefs*, which is a very remote Part in the
" *North* of *Scotland*, and we went immediate-
" ly to the (pretended) King of *England*, who
" Entertain'd the Motion with Joy, and
" told us, *We ought to Concert together the*
                                        Meafures

*Meaſures that were to be taken, and he would pur-
ſue our Reſolutions.*

" The Queſtion now was to get Pilots to
" Conduct us thither, and give us the neceſſary
" Notice : But there being none in our Squa-
" dron that was acquainted with that Port,
" Monſieur *de Fourbin* detach'd a Frigate, with
" the Sieurs *Caron* and *Bouyn*, to fetch ſome
" from the *Cape of Buccaneſs.* All that Day
" (25) we ſteer'd with a pretty favourable
" Wind towards the *North of Scotland*, but
" about Eleven at Night, there aroſe a ſtrong
" contrary Wind, which having continued
" the next Day with Violence, Monſieur *de*
" *Fourbin* told me, it was high time to acquaint
" the (pretended) King with the Inconveni-
" ences of purſuing our Courſe, which were
" the inevitable Diſperſion of our Fleet, the
" Danger the Ships that ſhould be ſeparated
" would be in, either of falling into the Ene-
" mies Hands, or of Periſhing on the Coaſt, if
" they were driven thither, and even the
" want of Proviſions.

" The impoſſibility the Sieurs *Caron* and
" *Bouyn* found of approaching the Shoar, by
" reaſon of the ſtormy Weather, and conſe-
" quently of bringing Pilots to Guide us ;
" the Uneaſineſs and Danger of Landing in a
" Port we were Strangers to, and where
" the Enemy might come up again with
" us, together with other Hazards and Diffi-
" culties, having been repreſented to the (pre-
" tended) King by Monſieur *de Fourbin*, in the
" Preſence of the Duke of *Perth*, my Lord
" *Middleton*, Mr. *Hamilton*, my Lord *Galmoy*,
" and Meſſieurs *de Beaharnois* and *d' Andrezel*,
" the

" the (pretended) King of *England*, with the
" unanimous Advice of all thofe Gentlemen
" refolv'd to return to *Dunki-k*, where could
" not arrive before this Day, by the reafon of
" the Calms and contrary Winds.

I am, &c.

The following Letter was likewife wrote from Dunkirk, *by an Officer of Diftinction to his Friend
at* Paris.

Dunkirk, April 12 N S, 1707

" WE were in fuch a Hurry on our Expe-
" dition to *Scotland*, the Defign being
" Communicated to none but our Prince's
" Privy Council till were on our March, that
" I neither could nor durft fay any thing of it,
" but now we are return'd I believe it won't
" be difagreeable to you to know the Truth
" of the Matter.
" When the Prince fet Sail, three Battalli-
" ons and fome Provifions that could not be
" got ready to go with him, were order'd to
" follow him to *Leith Road*, which accordingly
" we did four Days after, in Seven Privateers,
" Commanded by Monfieur *Zouft*, and got to
" *Leith Road* without meeting any Ships in
" our Paffage. We were much furpriz'd to
" find no Ships at our Place of Rendezvous
" and therefore put out *Dutch* Colours, and
" went clofe in with the Town of *Leith*, to
" get Intelligence. A Boat came of to u
" with two Pilots, who told us, that th
" *French* Fleet had not been there, but tha
" Advic

" Advice was come from the *Englifh* Fleet,
" which lay off the *Firth Mouth*, that the Peo-
" ple on Shoar took our Ships to be *Dutch*
" *Eaft-India Men*, that they heard had been
" upon the Coaft.

" We kept the Pilots on Board, and made
" all the hafte we could out of the *Firth*, kee-
" ping clofe under the *South* Shoar, to cover
" us from the fight of the *Englifh*, whom we
" faw off *Fifenefs*, about three Leagues to the
" Northward of us, fteering our Courfe *North
" Eaft*, we came up within two Days with
" the Body of the *French* Fleet, all fcatter'd,
" and refolving homeward. I went on
" Board the *Mars*, where I was told the
" Prince and Privy Council were, to receive
" further Orders, and give an Account of my
" Expedition, and there heard of their narrow
" Efcape, by the luckieft Accident in the
" World: They had got into the *Firth* on
" *Friday* Night, having heard nothing of the
" *Englifh* Fleet, and Anchor'd off *Pittenweem*
" and *Creil*, with Defign to Land near *Leith*
" in the Morning, when in the Night, they
" heard the *Englifh* Fleet fire the Signal for
" their Ships to come to an Anchor. Mon-
" fieur *Fourbin* knowing the meaning of it,
" immediately, fent a Boat on Board of every
" Ship in his Squadron, ordering them to put
" out their Lights, and to Sail one by one out
" of the *Firth*, and fteer a *North-Eaft* Courfe
" till they fhou'd come off the Town of St.
" *Andrew's*, which accordingly they did, but
" the Wind and Tide being againft them, the
" *Englifh* made them in the Morning and pur-
" fued them. In the Purfuit, which lafted
" three

" three Days, they loft the *Salisbury*, the
" *Blackwall* foundred fince at Sea, the *Deal,*
" *Caftle, Sun,* and *Squirrel* we are afraid are
" loft on the Coaft of *Holland,* and the *Tri-*
" *umph,* which we thought alfo loft is got in,
" but much fhatter'd. On *Thurfday,* put juft
" off of *Zealand,* our fmall Squadron fell in
" with four *Englifh* third Rates, which fright-
" ed us out of our Wits, for we were in fo dif-
" mal a Condition, that we could not make
" any Defence, and we muft have furrender'd;
" but they knowing nothing of our Circum-
" ftances bore away from us, and we got that
" Afternoon into *Dunkirk* Road, and next
" Day our Prince arriv'd with the reft in fo
" miferable a Condition all of us, that the
" Soldiers when they crept on Shoar, look'd
" more like Rats than Men. The Prince fuf-
" fer'd much in his Health, and what with
" Fatigue and Chagrin look'd very thin, but
" to put a good Face on the Matter, Drefs'd
" himfelf very fine, in an Embroider'd Suit,
" and a blue Feather in his Hat; when he went
" afhoar, where he was receiv'd by abundance
" of Ladies in their Coaches, with Looks that
" put me in Mind of an *Englifh* Funeral. When
" he went off the Noife was all over, *Long live*
" *the King*; but at our return fhrugging of
" Shouldiers and fhaking of Heads gave a dif-
" mal Welcome. Poor *Clermont* and his Bro-
" ther are taken in the *Salisbury,* and my Lord
" *Dumbarton* is either with them or loft in the
" *Blackwall.* General *Dorington, Gilmoy,* and
" fome of our Bottle Friends, are now very
" ill at Mr. *Gff*'s Houfe here, the *Macdonald's*
" *&c.* are gone up to St. *Germans* with the
" Prince.   I

" I need not tell you that the Foundation
" of our whole Defign was the Caftle of
" *Edinburgh*, which mifcarrying by the Arri-
" val of the *Englifh* Fleet, the Prince's Coun-
" cil did not think fit to land any where elfe.
" The Plan of this Caftle was laid before a
" Council of General Officers at *Verfailles*,
" and it was unanimoufly concluded, that with
" the Troops, Mortars, and Bombs, which
" we carry'd it could not hold above 3 Days.
" We defign'd to have made a Falfe Attack at
" at the Poftern Gate, while 3 Battallions
" fhould enter the Outworks that front the
" City, and lodge under their Half Moon,
" which would oblige them the next day to
" furrender. By the Taking of this Caftle
" we fhould have had the *Regalia* ; and I am
" told, Two *Proteftant* Archbifhops would
" have crowned the Prince in the High Church.
" The Equivalent from *England* being alfo in
" this Caftle, wou'd have been a great Supply
" to us for raifing of Men. We have above
" 400 Officers with us for that purpofe, all
" Pretty Fellows, that have ferv'd in the
" Wars of *Italy* and *Spain*, and above 100
" Chefts of Money. Some were for landing in
" *Murray Firth*, if it had been only to refrefh
" our Troops, but you know how nicely the
" *French* King's Orders are to be obey'd, and
" how little Power he gives of his Troops to
" any Ally, but always fecret ones to his own
" Generals We *Scots* and *Irifh* might have
" landed, but the *French* were reftrain'd to
" *Muffelbrough* and *Leith*, or no where.
To thefe Accounts, we fhall on the other
hand fubjoin, thofe that were written by Sir

K

George

George Bing, from on board the *Medway*, the
13th and 15th of *March*, O. S. The First
whereof is as follows. " According to the
" Opinion we had framed when we left the
" Station of *Dunkirk*, it has proved that the
" Enemy was defign'd for *Edinburgh*. This
" Morning we faw the *French* Fleet in the
" Mouth of the *Firth*, off of which Place we
" anchor'd the Laft Night, and fent a Boat
" afhore to the Ifle of *May*, from whence we
" had an account that the *French* came to an
" anchor yefterday in the Afternoon: They
" fent One Ship up into *Leith* Road, which
" had a Flag at the Main Topmaft Head : They
" report it a Blew one, but we are rather of
" opinion that it is the Standard. The People
" of the Ifland fay, that by the time that
" Ship could get up before the Town, they
" heard feveral Guns fire, which were in the
" manner of a Salute. The Ship that went
" up yefterday, came down this Morning,
" and is now within Two Leagues of us: She
" appears to be a Ship of 60 Guns, but has
" now no Flag on board We faw this
" Morning, when they weigh'd, a Flag at the
" Main-Top-Maft Head, on board of one of
" their Ships. They ftand from us, and we
' after them with all the fail we can.

    The Second Letter was as follows, " We
" chas'd the Enemy to the Northward of *Buc-*
" *canefs*, fometimes with reafonable Hopes of
" coming up with them The *Dover* and *Lud-*
" *low Caftle* being the only Clean-Sailing Ships
" we had : They were the firft which came up
" with part of the Enemies Squadron, paffing
" by fome of the Smaller to engage fome of
               " the

" the Larger Ships, and ſtop them till they
" ſhould be relieved. They attack'd 2 or 3
" of their Ships, amongſt which was the *Salis-*
" *bury :* They did not part with them till more
" of our Ships arriv'd, but work'd their Ships
" in a handſome manner, to cut them off
" from the reſt of the Fleet; but in the Dark-
" neſs of the Night they all got out of our
" Sight, except the *Salisbury,* who falling in
" amongſt our headmoſt Ships, the *Leopard* en-
" ter'd Men on board her. We were inform'd
" by the Officers who were taken, that there
" were 12 Battallions on board their Squadron,
" commanded by the Count *de Gace,* a Mar-
" ſhal of *France,* the pretended Prince of
" *Wales,* Lord *Middleton,* Lord *Perth,* the
" *Macdonalds, Trevanion,* and ſeveral other Of-
" ficers and Gentlemen on board the *Mars,* in
" which alſo was Monſieur *Fourbin,* who com-
" manded the Squadron. The Number and
" Strength of their Ships are very near the
" Account we lately received from *Dunkirk,*
" nor were they join'd by the *Breſt* Men of
" War. And they further aſſure us that the
" Ships our out Scouts ſaw off of *Calais,* were
" Privateers and their Prizes going into *Dun-*
" *kirk.* The Morning after this Chace, we
" ſaw but 18 of the Enemies Ships as far as
" we could perceive them from the Maſt-head,
" in the E N E of us Having no proſpect of
" coming up with them, we lay off and on
" *Buccaneſs* all Day yeſterday, to gather all our
" Ships together; and this day it blowing
" hard at N E with a Great Sea, judging the
" Enemy could not ſeize the Shore to make any
" attempt, we bore up for this Place, which

K 2 " was

" was thought moſt reaſonable, not only to
" ſecure, but to give Countenance and Spirit
" to Her Majeſty's Faithful Subjects, and diſ-
" courage thoſe that could have Thoughts of
" being our Enemies.

There were taken on Board the *Saliſbury*, the Lords *Griffin* and *Clermont*, Colonel of a Regiment, and Son to the Earl of *Middleton*, with Mr. *Middleton* his Brother, and Colonel *Francis Wanchup*; together with the Marquiſs *de Levy*, a *French* Lieutenant General, one aid de Camp, one Colonel, two Lieutenant Colonels, five Captains, two *French* Lieutenants, Fifteen *Iriſh* Lieutenants, ten Serjeants, ten Corporals, ten Lanſpeſſades, with M. *de Segent*, Commiſſary of War; and about 180 Soldiers. Beſides the Ships Company of about 300 Men, Officers included. As for the four firſt mention'd, as well as the fifteen *Iriſh* Lieutenants, being Subjects of *Great Britain*, they were brought to *London*, and Committed, the former to the *Tower*, and latter to *Newgate*. Many State Priſoners were likewiſe brought from *Edinburg* to *London*, who had been confin'd in the Caſtle of *Edinburgh*, and that were admitted to Bail, except ſuch againſt whom there was any particular Information, which I think was very few, not one Perſon having ſuffer'd on this Account. The Lord *Griffin* indeed was ſentenc'd upon a former Outlawry for High Treaſon, a Rule of Court was made out for his Execution, and a Warrant paſs'd for fulfilling the ſame, but he was repriev'd the Night before the Sentence ſhou'd have been Executed, and in the End died in the *Tower*

on the 10th of *November*, 1710.   And now
Sir *George Bing* having continu'd in *Leith
Road*, till he had Intelligence the *French* Fleet
was return'd to *Dunkirk*, he return'd to the
Downs, and thus ended this memorable Expedition, which had put *Britain* into a thou-
fand Hopes and Fears.   It is therefore time
to pursue the *Chevalier*, who was by this
time return'd to *France*.

The Gentleman who wrote one of the foregoing Letters from *Dunkirk*, seems to be mi-
ftaken, when he says the *Chevalier* return'd to
St. *Germans*, for he went from *Dunkirk* to St.
Omers, where he spent some time among the
English Gentlemen there, who in the Welcome
they gave him, cou'd not but mix with sad
and dejected Looks, some Sighs and affectionate Expressions of Sorrow, for the unfortunate Disappointment he had met with: But
he had learn'd so much of the Hero, as to shew
a perfect Unconcernedness at what they said,
and with a becoming Serenity, very rare in one
so young, turn'd the Discourse to other things.

The Armies being now ready to take the
Field in *Flanders*, he besought the *French* King
that he might serve among his Troops there,
then Commanded by the Dukes of *Burgundy*
and *Vendosme*, which the King not only comply'd with, but permitted the Duke of *Berry*
to accompany him.   They arriv'd in the Army some Days before the Battle of *Audenarde*,
in which the *Chevalier* was present during the
whole Action, and did the Duty of Aid de
Camp to the Duke of *Burgundy*, whom he conftantly attended during the heat of the Day.
Not only the *Paris Gazette*, and other *French*
News

News Papers, gave large Accounts of the in-
trepid Behaviour of the young Princes, but
Officers who were on the Spot cou'd not refrain speaking of it in their Letters, tho' they
were writ in very great Hury and Perplexity;
Which because they are not Foreign to the
Subject of these Memoirs, as well as that they
give a Concise Account of the Action, it wou'd
seem a Neglect to overlook them.

A Letter written by a French Officer, the Day after the Battle of *Andenard*.

I Can only send you the unwelcome Relation of the
Particulars of the Battle, which happen'd yester-
day about two in the Afternoon near Audenarde.
'I will prove a great Blow to France; for without
Exaggerating the Matter, we had above 10000
Men kill'd, wounded, or taken　The Action was
very ill manag'd on our side; for instead of attac-
king the Enemy when they began to pass the Schelde
near Audenarde at Eleven in the Morning, we let
them come over the River quietly, which they wou'd
not have adventur'd to do, had we in any tolerable
Manner offer'd to dispute their Passage; but seeing
us stand still, they were encourag'd to prosecute their
first Design, and began to pass over two Bridges
which they had laid. As fast as their Horse and
Foot came over, they rang'd themselves in Order of
Battle against us, and while our Generals were in
Suspence, what Resolutions to take, whether to ven-
ture an Engagement or not, the Enemy's Army continu'd coming over the River, and soon possess'd themselves of some Villages and Hedges; so that at last
our Generals were compell'd to endeavour to dislodge
them　Accordingly, our Infantry advanc'd, and
the Ground was disputed two or three Hours, with

a

a terrible Fire and great Obstinacy on both sides; but our Foot being tired with Charging the Enemy five or six times, and Dishearten'd to see themselves not supported by our Horse, (who cou'd not act because the Ground was so full of Inclosures) and press'd hard by the Enemy, were at length forc'd to retire, and quit the Ground to them. We Dragoons were oblig'd to endure the continual Fire of the Enemies Foot and Cannon, without daring to stir, because we were on the Right of the King's Houshold, who suffer'd as much as we. Toward the Evening, we were fallen upon by a great Number of the Enemy's Horse, to hinder us from succouring the rest, who were put to the Rout, and of Seven Regiments of Dragoons, we lost above half. At last, we saw no other Expedient, but to force our way thro' the Enemy; but first we sent to see whether we cou'd be assisted in that Design by any of our Forces In the mean time Night came on apace, and we were inform'd that the King's Houshold (whose Retreat was cover'd in some measure by us) were at too great a Distance. Things standing thus, our Resolution of breaking thro' the Enemy sunk, and some of the Enemy's Adjutants summoning us to yield our selves Prisoners of War, we submitted to it, seeing no other way to save our Lives. At least Forty of our Regiments are reduced to a wretched Condition, the greatest part of them being kill'd or taken, so that it will be long before they can be Re-establish'd. Of four Regiments of the King's Houshold, at least half were taken Prisoners, and among them are several Persons of Note. The Chevalier de Longville, and 15 other Officers were mortally wounded, and two of them are since dead. The Regiments of Pfiffer and Villars are quite ruin'd, and almost all their Officers are taken, with all their Baggage, &c. The

The Dukes of Burgundy, Berry, *and the* Chevalier de St. George, *staid at the Head of the Houshold during the whole Action, and Retreated with them to* Ghent, *where we are just now told they are safe arriv'd. I cannot pretend to tell you yet what the Result of this Battle will be, or how our Generals will square their Motions, which we are like to have no farther Share in this Campaign.*

Yours,

Another Letter had in it this Expression.

That there was not wanting those, who advis'd the Princes to set out Post for Ipres, *but this they generously refus'd, and staid at the Head of the Troops till the very last.* And the Duke de *Vendosme* in his Letter to the King of *France*, assur'd him, *That the* Chevalier de St. George, *and the Duke* de Berry, *were very forward and active during the Battle.*

The next Summer, the *Chevalier* made the Campaign under the Marshal *de Villars*, who had a particular Charge of him, and with whom during the whole time of continuing in the Field, he constantly accompany'd on all Duties, and rode with him continually when he visited the Lines, or Recoroitred the Enemy, and in the Battle of *Mons*, or *Blaregnies*, was present with him in the Heat of all the Action, as we may find by the Marshal *de Boufler* Account thereof to the King, where he has these Words, in the Conclusion of his Letter, applied to the Behaviour of those that Distinguish'd themselves in the Battle.

I

I Cannot now give Your Majesty any particulars of this Action, but will endeavor to send 'em to morrow, or next day: I can assure Your Majesty that all the General Officers did their Duty perfectly well, and with the greatest Bravery and Skill; but Monsieur d'Artagnan, who commanded the Right of the Foot, distinguish'd himself in a particular manner, as well by this Valor as by his good Orders: He had 3 Horses kill'd under him, and received 4 Blows on his Cuirass: The D. de Guiche, who was also on the Right, a little forwarder than M. D'Artagnan, behav'd himself with all possible Skill and Bravery, and received a Musket Shot in his Leg: The Marquis Damfort and M. de la Frazeliere, who were also on the Right, and in M. d'Artagnan's Rear, shewed the same Valor and Capacity: M. de Gassion, who commanded the Right Wing of Horse, did Wonders at the Head of your Majesty's Houshold, and shew'd on this Occasion his Courage and Ability, having push'd and defeated more than 2 or 3 of the Enemies Lines Sword in Hand. The Gendarmes, Light Horse, Musqueteers, and Horse Grenadiers also did Wonders. The P. de Rohan, and M. de Vidame did all that could be expected from Persons of the greatest Valor: The Gendarmerie did Wonders also, and the Marquis de la Valiere was every where, and charged with all possible Bravery at all the different Charges. The Cavalry behaved themselves very well, and all the Troops, as well as the Foot, stood with incredible Firmness one of the briskest Canonades that ever was. All the Foot did Wonders and distinguish'd them.

The Chevalier De St. George behaved himself, during the whole Action, with all possible Bravery and Vivacity I say nothing of Your Majesty's Left, by reason I was not there, but I know that all the General Officers, and all the Troops, animated by the Mareschal de Villars's Presence and Example, behaved themselves with all possible Valor

Upon his Return from this Campaign, the Chevalier was complimented by the Principal of the Court of France, for the Mareschal de Villars had likewise given such an account, as serv'd to heighten the public Opinion of him.　　　L　　　I

I am now, for want of more Room, drawing to a Conclusion of these Memoirs. And it may be well presum'd there are many things that will not bear mentioning, with regard to the Strictness of Caution we are now ty'd up to. As there is no Offence design'd, so I cannot but suppose there will be none taken. Were he of no other Consideration but his adding a Clause (and perhaps one of the most considerable) in the whole Articles of this memorable Treaty for Peace, it seems sufficient to warrant an Undertaking of this nature, and to record a NAME in some collected manner, that is, and indeed but barely is, scatter'd and interspers'd thro' so many Scraps of History. I shall only further remember the Reader, that Last Year he made a tour thro' the Eastern Parts of *France*, while at the same time there was a great Armament at *Toulon* and *Brest*; which amus'd a considerable part of *Europe*, and gave foundation to a Surmise, that some Expedition was to be made in his Favor.

He had before had an interview with the *French* King, who in a very solemn manner, tho' not without Impressions of Concern, told him, that he found himself under the necessity of giving Peace to his People, and that some Overtures had pass'd which gave him hopes of obtaining that long desir'd End: He propos'd therefore to him many Places for his Retreat, which he was assur'd must attend the issue of the Affair. But remember'd to him what he had formerly said on this Subject, from which he assur'd him he shou'd never alter.

He visited most of the Principal Towns of that Part of *France*, and likewise the Army of the Duke *de Berwick*. But as there was a good space of Time, in which the Public News gave no account of his Journey, it confirms me in the Opinion of what I have been confidently told, That he then visited the Place of his Retreat, when he quits the Realms of *France*, and had a private interview with a certain Prince that is to receive him.

The

The beginning of *April* laft, a few Days after his (suppos'd) Sifter, he was vifited with the Small Pox, and in great Danger of Death, but Providence défign'd to lengthen a LIFE, tho' meanly treated in Hiftory, that has a very large fhare in the moft momentuous Affairs that relate to this part of *Europe*, and wou'd yet be of more Regard were not *France* reduc'd to the Neceffity of fubmitting, that the Prefervation of their National Religion in *Britain*, is the moft juft and 'reafonable part of their Government, and which to fubvert, will not only be the moft difficult thing in Nature, but always preferr'd above the Concern for their Lives and fafety

I Conclude all with an Account of the Death and Character of the Princefs *Louifa Maria Terefa*, Daughter of King *James* II who died of the Small Pox at *St. Germains*, the 18th of *April* 1712 as it was faid to be fent in a Letter from a Nobleman of *France*, to his Correfpondent at *Utrecht*.

MY LORD,

I *Send you by thefe, the fad and deplorable News of the much lamented Death of the Princefs Royal of* England, *who died of the Small-Pox, the* 18th *of this Month, at* St Germains, *who as fhe was one of the greateft Ornaments of that afflicted Court, fo fhe was the Admiration of all* Europe, *never Princefs was fo univerfally regretted. Her Death has filled all* France *with Sighs, Groans, and Tears. She was a Princefs of a majeftical Mien and Port, every Motion fpoke Grandeur, every Action was eafy and without any Affectation or Meannefs, and proclaim'd her a Heroine defcended from the long Race of fo many Peternal and Maternal Heroes, Majefty fat enthron'd on her Forehead, and her curious large black Eyes ftruck all that had the Honour to approach her, with Awe and Reverence; but all her External Glories, though the greateft*

of

of her Sex, were nothing to her Internal, and she seems to have establish'd the Opinion of Plato, who asserts, That the Soul frames its own Habitation, and that beautiful Souls make to themselves beautiful Bodies. *She had a great deal of pleasant Wit, joined with an equal Solidity of Judgment; she was Devout, without the Defects that young Aspirers to Piety are sometimes incident to; and though she comply'd with the Diversions of the Court, her greatest Pleasure was in pious Retirement. She was very affable, and of a sweet mild Temper, full of Pity and Compassion, which is the distinguishing Character of the Royal Family of the* Stuarts. *To sum up all in a few Words, she was a dutiful and obedient Daughter, an affectionate Sister, tenderly loving and belov'd by the Hero her Brother On both their Countenances were divinely mingled the noble Features and Lineaments of the* Stuarts *and the* D' Este's, *and Beauty triumph'd over both, with this only Difference, That in him it was more Strong and Masculine as becoming his Sex, in her more Soft and Tender as more suiting with hers; in both, excellent and alike. She was four Years younger, as if designed by Providence to confute the black Calumny of her Brother's Birth, and her Royal Mother's Inability of having Children To be short, in her the Distressed have lost a certain Comforter, her Servants an excellent Mistress, and the World one of its most precious Gems She died expressing the warmest Sentiments of Piety, and the most perfect Resignation, uttering often her Royal Father's dying Words and Ejaculations, as Inheritrix of his Piety. The great Discomposure of my Mind on this sad Occasion, and my gushing Tears hinder me to add any more. Adieu.*

FINIS.

9 781170 505069